The Million Dollar Writer

HOW TO HAVE A LEGITIMATE – AND LUCRATIVE – CAREER AS A WRITER

Richard S. Gallagher

Contents

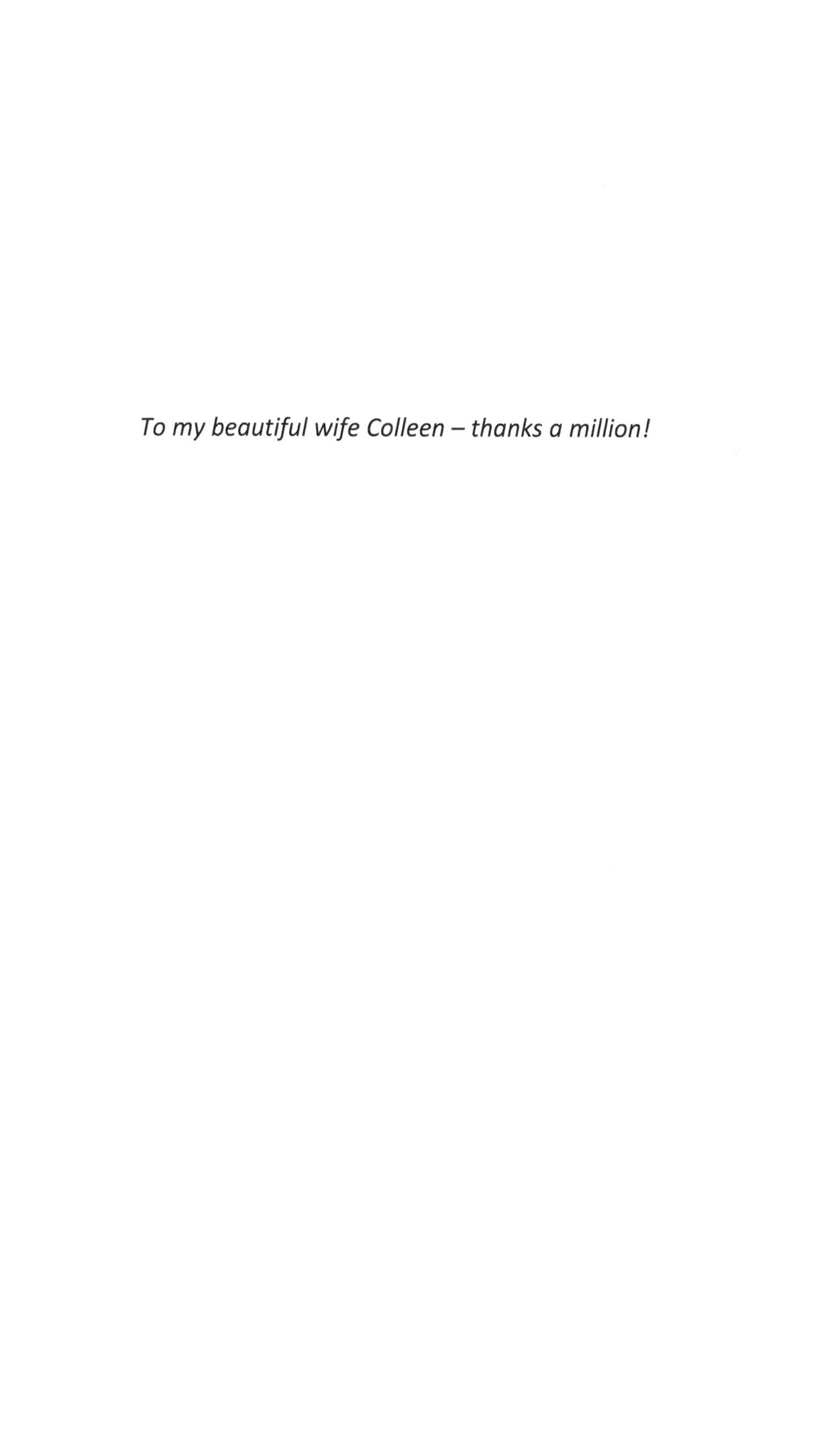

To my beautiful wife Colleen – thanks a million!

It's none of their business that you have to learn to write. Let them think you were born that way.

— Ernest Hemmingway

Introduction

will be honest with you: I thought long and hard about the title of this book. Why? Because the phrase "Million Dollar Writer" sounds so ... get-rich-quick-y.

In reality, though, that phrase describes my life pretty accurately. I have sold over a million dollars worth of books as an author. I have earned more than a million dollars writing for other people. And I have earned close to another million dollars speaking to audiences about my books. So yes, I really am a million dollar writer. And I honestly believe that you can become one too.

But if you are looking for how to make a million dollars *quickly*, this isn't your book. I am here to teach you how to have a comfortable, professional living as a writer. One that pays mortgages, buys new cars, provides health insurance coverage, and is dependable from year to year. And a life that opens up a lot of possibilities compared with almost any other profession, for all sorts of people including:

- Students supplementing their income
- Professionals moonlighting while they are still working
- Stay-at-home parents having a very legitimate career while being with their kids
- People starting their careers over at midlife
- Above all, making a real living doing one of the most fun things imaginable: writing

In short, this is a book on how to have the kind of life I have lived for a long time. If that is the kind of writer you want to be, read on.

When people find out that I am a writer, they usually ask me two things. The first is what my day job is. (In reality, I have supported my household as a writer for many years.) The second thing they ask is the same thing I wanted to know 20 years ago – how do I become a successful one?

Glad you asked. People mistakenly believe that the world is neatly divided into one very small and privileged group of Those Who Are Writers and a much larger group of Those Who Are Not. They feel that some people are born with a silver pen in their hand, or have the right connections, or are somehow just lucky, while the rest of us are doomed to a life among the underemployed and unpublished masses.

In reality, nothing is further from the truth. These assumptions are certainly not true for me personally. I was not a born writer. In fact, I was a C student in writing in college, and did not become a full-time writer until midlife (after running screaming from the corporate world for the last time). I did not have great publishing connections, but rather was a humble lay middle manager by the time I landed my first book contract. And as for being lucky, I know better: both my publishers and my clients often tell me that they choose to work with me because I am really good at what I do.

So first and foremost, my goal is to have you look at writing in terms of two very different categories of people: Those Who Follow the Process and Those Who Do Not. Because there is a logical process to writing successfully for a living. In my experience, most people who follow it eventually succeed, and most people who do not follow it don't. Once you learn this process, there is no reason you cannot succeed as well. And the purpose of this book is to lay out this process for you, step by step.

Being a writer is a great life AND a great career. And, surprisingly, most truly good writers will tell you that there are not enough of us out there, and there is always room in the profession for many more. My goal here is to open my playbook and teach you the same secrets that made me a success. And, I truly hope and believe, help you become a million dollar writer yourself.

What this book will teach you

Do you know what one of my biggest pet peeves is? Self-help books that have "too much sauce and not enough steak." Particularly when they pither from one chapter of background information to the next before, somewhere on page 247, they finally get to the meat of what you purchased the book for- sort of. So my goal here is to give you a summary, up front, of the key take-aways you will learn here. Then you can hop, skip and jump through the book as you please.

First, let's start with the basic premise of the book: over the next decade or so of your life, earning a million dollars as a writer or selling a million dollars' worth of books is a very rational and reasonable goal as long as (a) you already write reasonably well, (b) you love to write, and (c) you follow the lead of the marketplace.

Steps (a) and (b) are important, because to earn a million dollars you will do a *lot* of writing. If you aren't already reasonably good, and you don't love the smell of newly minted prose, the amount of writing you will need to do to get there will seem exhausting and insurmountable. If you can look in the mirror and smile at the prospect of eventually writing roughly 4000 words per week, each and every work week, welcome to the club. (If you cannot, put this book down now and back away slowly.)

However, it is step (c) that truly separates the million dollar writers from the wannabes. Following the lead of the marketplace sounds healthy, logical and rational – however, the vast majority of writers never do it. Let's break this down, for both freelance writers and book authors:

- Many people who write well do not understand the mechanics of creating work that is professional and publishable. We will break this difference down for you in detail.
- Most people who call themselves "writers" think about writing articles and books. For most people, however, these are low-paying, labor intensive markets and not a middle-class living.

- "Boring" writing markets tend to be lucrative AND understaffed. I have made hundreds of thousands of dollars writing manuals for manufacturers, scientific articles for government publications, and blog posts and white papers for corporations. And all of it sharpens my axe for my own published writing.

- The key to successfully landing clients is the same as the key to success in baseball: "hit the ball where they ain't." Mass-market magazines generally have sky-high slush piles. Major media outlets generally source content on a don't-call-us-we'll-call-you basis. But at the same time, right at this very moment, there are people out there who are desperate to find good, dependable writers – at temp agencies, software companies, widget manufacturers, government agencies, universities, and a host of other places. We'll explore this hidden job market for writers in detail.

- Next, we will turn our attention to book publishing. For most nonfiction authors there is no comparison, market-wise, between writing royalty published books for major publishers (which tend to sell in the thousands) versus self-published books (which often require really strong sales channels and marketing strategies to sell more than dozens). There are exceptions, of course. But for most people, if you want to sell a million dollars' worth of books – about 4-5 thousand books per year over the next dozen years – getting good enough to be royalty published is the quickest way to get there. And as this book will lay out in detail, this is a more reachable goal than you might think.

- Less than 5% of book proposals submitted to many major publishers or agents ever get accepted. But there is an important reason for this: more than half of them STINK. We will explore the reasons for this later, but for now, the important point is that if you write an appropriate proposal and multiply it by the number of appropriate publishing channels that are out there, your chances rise to a much more reasonable 50/50 or so in my view.

- Writing successfully and professionally opens the door to many other lucrative streams of income, including workshops, coaching, speaking, and information products.

The message of this book is that a good living as a writer is not only possible, but extremely practical and attainable. My goal here is to open the playbook that I and many other successful writers have used to get there. All that I ask in return is that you bring an open mind along on this journey, because I plan to challenge many of your beliefs about the writing life along the way. From here, we will explore a wealth of practical strategies for becoming a million-dollar writer, chapter by chapter.

Finally, a few caveats. First, we will be focusing on non-fiction writing and not fiction. (Although one of my biggest selling books was, in fact, a book of fictional business fables.) Being a good fiction writer is a great skill, and potentially lucrative in its own right, but not my expertise – moreover, the vast majority of commercial writing markets involve non-fiction. Second, a common theme here will be following the market rather than your muse: if you are looking to make a million dollars writing about *your* subjects, this book may disappoint you. Finally, like any worthwhile endeavor in life, your ultimate success will be directly proportional to the work you put in long after you put down this book.

I truly love writing. I love taking ideas, putting them on paper, and molding and shaping them in a voice that is much more worldly and interesting than I could ever be in person. Making a career of it is a pleasure and a privilege that I feel is open to the many, not just the few. Join me and discover your own lucrative path to the writing life.

CHAPTER 1

The One Big Secret of Freelance Writing

I wish I had a dollar for every time that I sat across from someone who said to me, "I wish I could make a living as a writer, but there is no money in it."

Usually I would politely respond that I actually made a very good living as a writer, and that I feel it is a very good profession to work in. To which they would often respond with statements like:

"Sure, that's nice, but you were lucky."

"The system is rigged against most people."

"Most people couldn't do that."

"My Aunt Mildred tried to write and didn't get anywhere."

And then there is my personal favorite, "Well, it's not like you're a bestselling author or anything." (Actually, I am a bestselling author. But we'll save that for a later chapter.)

So what is the difference between these people and me? And all the other people I know who make a good living as writers? Aside from a negative attitude and self-limiting beliefs, I believe their problems are simple: they don't understand the real secret behind being a successful freelance writer – one who builds a steady stream of high-value writing assignments and clients, and for whom writing provides a secure upper-middle-class living.

The secret of freelance writing

So what is this secret? I don't like suspense any more than you do, so here it is:

Boring is better.

Repeat this over and over to yourself. Tape it to your mirror if you want. But whatever you do, always remember: *boring is better*. Because the less glamorous a market is, the more lucrative and successful it is to write for. All sorts of good things happen when you write for these so-called "boring" markets:

- The barriers to entry are lower
- The competition is smaller
- The compensation is much better
- The marketing process is simpler
- Your chances of landing solid, long-term clients go up substantially

Think about it: at this very moment, three people are sitting at identical word processors, writing identical amounts of verbiage. One is writing a query for an article for a major magazine with a sky-high slush pile. It will never get accepted. Another is writing a blog post for a trendy niche consumer blog. She will receive a token payment that might cover her next trip to Starbucks. Meanwhile, the third is writing a marketing blog for a software company and earning $70 an hour – and will be writing blogs like this for them all year.

This secret is nothing more than the law of supply and demand, and it is never truer than in the writing life. Yet when many if not most people think about making a living from writing, they instinctively head for places that will never sustain them. They submit articles to major magazines, they try to monetize their blogs, or they approach their local paper about writing a feature. Or they search for gigs on freelance websites that are already overwhelmed with low-paid offshore competitors. They earn nickel-and-dime levels of compensation. And eventually they wonder why they can't make a go of a writing career, and give up.

By comparison, let's look at some of the ways I've made money writing over the years. Here is a sample of just a few of my gigs:

- Creating the operating and service manuals for a line of specialty printers.
- Transcribing and editing the talks for an academic conference.
- Developing course materials for software companies.
- Editing academic papers and doctoral theses.
- Creating web content for a number of health care clients.
- Writing specialty medical articles for pharmaceutical industry clients.
- In one of my biggest ongoing engagements I earned over a quarter of a million dollars writing about tobacco tax policy for government publications. And no, I am not an expert in it. (Although I know a lot more about it than I did before!)

This isn't to say that all my writing is boring – or that all of yours will be. Some of my paid projects have been very cool. For example, I did a children's book parody for a New York advertising firm that was eventually narrated on YouTube by a major movie star. I've published articles for *Time Magazine*, CNN, and many other major markets. And, as we will discuss in later chapters, I've ghostwritten several nationally-published books as well as writing several under my own byline, two of which were major-category bestsellers. And frankly, I would be the first to admit that all of my professional writing helped sharpen my axe for my more publicly visible work.

First let's define "boring" writing, as it applies to your writing career:

It has a niche audience. A blog article on, say, how to get a date – or deal with a difficult boss – has a wide audience of both readers and potential writers. (Which is precisely why demand levels and pay rates for such pieces are often terrible.) By comparison, a manual for how to set an alarm clock is only of interest to people who purchase that alarm clock. But that manual still needs to be there, and someone needs to write it.

It has limited interest to the general consumer. In general, most people don't care about the settings for a niche software product. Or the content for a health care facility's website. Or the assembly instructions for a thermal printer. Or a two-day course on how to program telephone systems[1]. This works to your advantage, because the vast majority of writers don't seek to create content like this. And as you build your portfolio for projects like these, you will find yourself to be part of a small fraternity of people that are in very high demand.

It has high value to the client. Products cannot get released without instructions and documentation. They cannot get sold without sales and marketing copy. They cannot get fixed without manuals and specifications. People cannot get trained without courseware content. And the list goes on and on from there. While many general consumer-market essayists could frankly get sucked into a hole deep in the earth and never be missed, "boring" writers are VIPs who are well paid and mission-critical to their clients.

It requires getting your hands dirty. I want to be clear that "boring" writing is not just technical writing. (Although my examples may be a bit biased – I do have an engineering degree and have consulted for a lot of technical firms.) And you do NOT have to be an expert in what you are writing about. But most successful "boring" writing does require you to put yourself into the head of your client, and write from their perspective.

---

[1] All projects I have actually done, by the way.

I've sat down with engineers and watched them disassemble products, notepad in hand. I've flown across the country to listen to public health experts discuss policy issues, to produce a proposed outline for their next publication. I've even interviewed senior executives and famous scientists based halfway around the globe about their work, and written about it. To play in this arena, you don't have be technically oriented, or as smart as your clients – but you do have to be open to listening to and learning from them, and then put a literate and human face on what they do.

Its "cool factor" is low. Telling someone that you are a contributor to Cosmopolitan, or a Huffington Post blogger, or interview rock stars for a website, is definitely cool. And in many cases, highly competitive and grossly underpaid. By comparison, telling people that you edit farming reports may not make you a hit at parties – but you'll be much more likely to smile every time you look at your bank statement.

Here is why I feel so-called "boring" writing is exactly what you want to focus on, in your quest to become a professional writer:

- *It is perfectly designed for the gig economy*. Here is the key reason why "boring" writing is such a great field for freelancers: <u>it isn't a full-time need for many clients</u>. While some firms may be big enough to have one or more writers on staff, many others just need a quarter of a person, or a tenth of a person, to produce their written content. And even larger firms with their own writing staffs often have peak periods where they need outside help. If you can be that tenth of a person for ten clients, they are happy and you are happy.
- *It pays much better*. The essential on-demand nature of most business and professional writing means that you can command freelance rates for your work, which are often much better than what employees are paid. (Try hiring a plumber or an electrician for an entire week at their hourly freelance rate, and you will see what I mean.) This is why once you have regular clients, freelance writing is often a lucrative professional career.

- *The market is vast*. Walk or drive around your town sometime, and look at all the businesses that you see out there. Every single one of them — from a small law firm needing advertising brochures to a large manufacturer that publishes hundreds of documents — needs written content, without exception. Which means that your potential market stretches as far and as wide as you can cover.

- *The need is always there*. Once you get established in the field, few clients ever finish their last marketing piece, their last training course, or their last service manual. Professional writing tends to be a great source of recurring business as you gain clients and build a good reputation.

- *You aren't competing with bottom-feeders*. Nowadays, you can go on websites like Fiverr or Elance and find offshore freelancers who can afford to work for extremely low rates. If you serve the general consumer market, you are competing with these freelancers. But most businesses and professional clients aren't going to look on Fiverr for their written communications needs. They need quality and stability, and realize they have to pay for it.

- *The market doesn't care who you are*. Are you a stay-at-home parent who wants to spend more time with your kids? Or a late-career professional whose job prospects have become limited? Or someone who wants to create a legitimate, upper-middle-class career while living with a disability? Or someone who recently dropped out of college or graduate school? Guess what — if you write well and solve problems for people, no one cares how old you are, what you look like, or what your personal circumstances are.

  Some of my clients have never even seen me. They have no idea that I am a balding, 63-year-old man in upstate New York. They have never seen my resume or asked what my GPA is. For that matter, they don't know if I even attended college. (Although I do, in fact, have a masters degree.) All they know about me is my writing portfolio and my track record, or often just good word-of-mouth from other clients. Writing is often a perfect career for people who "color outside the lines" of traditional credentials.

- *It gives you a very flexible lifestyle.* This is perhaps the greatest secret of all about freelance professional writing – it can become a very stable living that gives you a great deal of freedom, something few other careers can offer.

When I was last in corporate life – many years ago – I had two weeks of vacation a year, my boss decided when I could take a day off, and I had to clock in to the same office every morning. As a writer I can live where I want, travel, or even take on additional sources of income. (As we will discuss later in this book, I ultimately added a lucrative practice of public speaking about my own books, and later fulfilled a lifelong dream of becoming a practicing psychotherapist – all while keeping very busy as a writer.) My only responsibilities are to my clients, and how I choose to live and do my job is completely up to me.

Personally, I have a very strong bias about freelance professional writing as a career: I feel it is one of the most stable ways to make a living. Ironically, many people view having a regular job as more secure, but not me. To me, having a single job that can get whacked at any time seems risky and crazy, while having a regular stable of well-paying clients feels sober and rational. For me – and I hope for you – a successful freelance writing practice has few equals in creating a comfortable, upper-middle-class living doing work that you really enjoy.

Putting the secret to work

To wrap up this section in one neat package: too often, the typical person who sets out to be a professional writer thinks about writing things like magazine articles, blog posts, or popular content – and in my experience, the vast majority of them starve. Or they put their name out there in online marketplaces for freelance writers, where they are competing with hundreds or even thousands of low-priced competitors, many of whom are based offshore. But this isn't what I want you to do.

I want you to be a legitimate, professional writer with a good career. And right now, in your town, there are lots of boring, unglamorous clients who desperately need people like you to write for them. From here, I will be pointing you towards how to find these clients and make yourself attractive to them. Never forget: boring is better.

I also want to be clear that this profession isn't for everyone. It is only for people who already basically write well – and more importantly, love to write. You will need at least a modicum of computer, internet and social media skills to succeed, along with the ability to work quickly. And like any freelance work, you will need the interpersonal skills to build and maintain great relationships with your clients.

No book, coach or training program can make these things happen. If your spell-checker goes crazy every time you sit down to write, you naturally communicate in text-message LOL-speak, you are deadline-challenged, or you have a hard time motivating yourself to express ideas in writing, this may not be your thing. That's OK. But the good news is that if you've got the basic skills and motivation, the mechanics of this profession can be learned.

In the chapters that follow, we are going to explore the two main ingredients for building a successful freelance writing career: learning how to smell like a professional writer, and learning how to market yourself. Let's get started!

CHAPTER 2

How to Write Like a Professional

News flash: to be a successful freelance writer, you must write well. And more important, you and your portfolio need to smell like that of a professional writer.

A great deal of this is on you, of course. I am presuming that you already write reasonably well, and are open to always trying to improve your craft. Now, here is where I come in. This chapter is going to go through a few simple hacks for your writing that will help you sound like a true professional – secrets of the trade that will set you apart from most other people.

Follow these simple rules, and you will have a high probability of sounding professional – and in turn, landing more clients and projects. Here we go:

Rule no. 1. Rock the opening

Your opening is the "hook" that makes the reader decide whether to invest his or her time in reading the rest of your piece. Good openings vary with the type of freelance writing you are doing, of course – an assembly manual will have a different opening than a sales letter, for example – but in general, your goal is to create a mental image the reader wants to learn more about.

This means that every word of your opening paragraphs is critically important, both for prospective clients and the audience for your writing. Here are some examples of techniques you can use to create good openings:

Ask a question: Start the piece by asking a question – rhetorical or otherwise – that the reader might want to hear an answer to. For example:

"How would you like to manage a workforce that thinks just like you do, cares about your company as much as you do, and who consistently goes above and beyond the standards you set for them?"

Create a counterpoint: Here you open the piece in the form, "You thought X, but Y happened."

For example, once I did an article (on very short notice) for *Time Magazine* in the wake of a customer service debacle – a customer named Ryan Block tried unsuccessfully for nearly 20 minutes to cancel his Comcast account, and his recording of the whole excruciating call went viral. So instead of simply stating this, my opening paragraph read as follows:

"Poor Ryan Block. He and his wife Veronica thought they would simply make a phone call to cancel their Comcast service when they switched providers. Instead, they went through a hellish 18-minute ordeal with an abusive "retention specialist" who browbeat both of them to keep their service. The result was a Kafka-esque conversation with a rep who continually held his powers of cancellation far out of reach."

Give a credentialing example. The book *The Wisdom of Crowds* has a truly great opening. It tells of how people tried to guess the weight of an ox, writing their guesses on slips of paper – and while no one guessed its weight correctly, the average of all the slips was almost its exact weight.

This is a perfect use of a credentialing example: a story or anecdote that makes your premise believable, and ideally creates an "a-ha" moment that the reader is going to learn something they never knew before. The whole point of *The Wisdom of Crowds* is that good decisions lie with the input of large numbers of people, and this amazing story nailed this point perfectly.

Tell a story. The best opening I have ever seen comes from another book example, *Just Listen* by Dr. Mark Goulston. Dr. Goulston is a psychiatrist who trains hostage negotiators for the FBI, and he starts his book by walking you step-by-step through what he says when someone has a gun to his own head in a parking lot. POW! Who wouldn't want to read further to find out what happens? And then the idea that you, the reader, can learn the same skills is irresistible. We learn facts, but we think in story form – use this to hook the reader about your piece's premise.

Speak to the reader's emotions. Which would be a better opening to a piece on marital communications skills: "Communications skills are important in a marriage" or "Megan was in tears again. And her husband George was trying to figure out why they could never talk about their sex life without it turning into a big fight." When you show instead of tell, using examples that readers themselves can relate to, they get emotionally involved with what you have to say.

These aren't the only good ideas for an opening, of course – your options are only limited by your imagination. No matter what technique you use, however, there is one goal for any opening – it should go POW and hook the reader. So if you are looking for the quickest way to be seen as a talented freelance writer, your reputation may be as close as your opening paragraphs.

Rule no. 2. You've got 30 seconds

What is the cardinal sin of most writers? Pithering back and forth about a topic without getting to the "meat" of it. Along with a good opening hook, your first couple of paragraphs or so should tell – or at least hint – about how your piece will benefit the reader, within the first 30 seconds. Why? Because this is about as long as a reader or reviewer will give you before deciding whether to read further.

This is a particular failing of much technical writing. I've made a great deal of my own living editing other people's technical publications, and a typical one starts off something like this:

> *Psoriasis is a major public health problem. Since it was first discovered in 1872, people have struggled with what they now call "the heartbreak of psoriasis", bla, bla, bla.*
>
> *Previous studies on psoriasis have shown that bla, bla, bla (Dull 1994, Boring 2003, Longwinded 2004). Other researchers have found bla, bla, bla. This has led to other studies, bla, bla, bla.*

And then, after several more paragraphs of blathering, they finally disclose what the actual paper is about – long after the reader has gone to sleep:

> *This paper discusses a survey of current physician attitudes toward the treatment of psoriasis. It looks at bla, bla, bla.*

I invariably do three things with articles like these:

- I move the last paragraph of the introduction (e.g. the paper or chapter purpose) to become the first one.
- I boil this section down to be no more than a manuscript page and a half in length, with short, clear paragraphs.
- I make sure that every sentence and every paragraph supports a clear purpose and outcome, and move the background and history to a subsequent section.

It is an accepted rule of thumb that you have no more than 30 seconds to make an impression – good or bad – on the person reading or reviewing your project. So think about how you will make the most of that critical first sentence, first paragraph, and first page, so that it serves as an "elevator speech" (i.e. what you would tell someone on a 30-second elevator ride) about what is new, different, and important with this publication.

Rule no. 3. Plan it out

One of the worst things you can do with a project is start writing on page one and continue to the end. Why? Because good professional nonfiction writing has a timing, pacing and rhythm that works best if you plan the flow of the document before you set finger to keyboard.

I often joke that I write with a calculator. But honestly, I do. If I am writing a corporate blog, I know it will run 500-600 words and have roughly 7-8 paragraphs. And that each of these paragraphs have a specific role, such as an opening hook, credentialing examples, body points, call to action and so forth. Likewise, a book chapter, a white paper, or a marketing brochure has a form and a function that I can plan ahead of time. And then my job becomes easy, familiar, and mechanical.

For larger projects, I sometimes create a visual "map" of the publication to help flesh it out into readable, high-impact content. This map is not necessarily published, but is used to plan my efforts and communicate with the client. Here is one example:

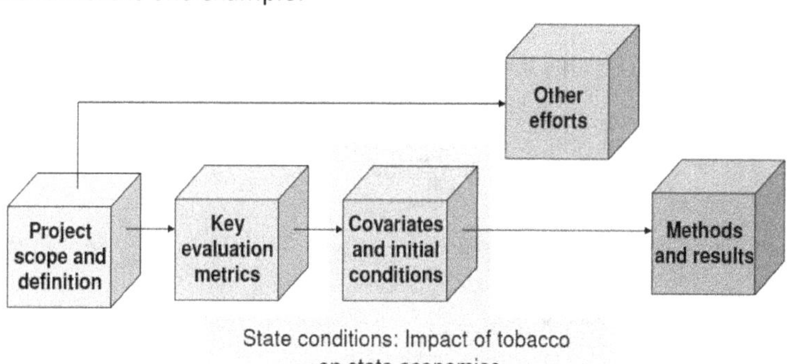

State conditions: Impact of tobacco on state economies

(Adapted from: National Cancer Institute. Evaluating ASSIST: A Blueprint for Understanding State-level Tobacco Control.Tobacco Control Monograph No. 17. Bethesda, MD: U.S. Department of Health and Human Services, National Institutes of Health, National Cancer Institute. NIH Pub. No. 06-6058, October 2006.)

The figure shown here is a section plan for a government monograph volume I was involved with. Note that it defines a logical order of sections, and more important, a sense of the flow from section to section, including one section outside this normal flow. Once we had consensus on this flow, this figure guided several months of writing efforts.

In much the same way, a plan for the sections of a publication helps frame its content, which brings me to the second most common thing that I do editing a technical paper: turning a deathless pile of content into a story with a beginning, a middle, and an end.

Finally, many published pieces are subject to word limits – either because of the guidelines of the publication, or because of the physical limitations of the medium (such as the size and layout of a brochure). One more important benefit to a good outline is that it helps you plan estimated word counts for each section. This lets you effectively strategize the level of detail and content you use, making this outline a game plan for a clear, effective publication.

Rule no. 4. Keep it short and keep it simple

You are probably highly intelligent. You may be highly educated. So what is your attention span as a reader? According to studies, less than five minutes – a figure that, in fact, may be much better than that of the audience who will actually be reading your publications.

This means that the single most productive thing you can do to create a readable piece is to think *short* – because we all read and understand short bursts of information much more easily than a "wall of words." Here are some guidelines:

- Paragraph lengths should ideally be no more than 80-100 words for general nonfiction – ideally less – and no more than 150 to 200 words for complex technical documents.
- Create sections and subsections so that none of your lowest level sections are more than two to three manuscript pages.
- For trade press and popular articles, use bullet items like these to outline key points and break up large blocks of text.

Within limits, the general rule is that the more you break things up, the merrier. And a general rule of thumb here is to try and write at an eighth-grade level.

Rule no. 5. Highlight the good stuff

What do you give your young children to read? Books with lots of pictures, games, and activities? Or an unabridged manuscript of *War and Peace*?

The reality is that your readers and reviewers are not that much different from children from a cognitive standpoint: we all like to be engaged and entertained. So aside from using short paragraphs and sections, using lots of "eye candy" – such as figures, tables, and sidebars – is the next most important thing you can do to insure reader interest and retention. (I am doing exactly the same thing here in this chapter!)

Sidebars are a great way to highlight important text, or interesting sidelights, in a way that breaks up your story and keeps the reader interested. Here is an example of one:

Sidebars and summaries: The low-budget, high-impact rewrite

For a major government monograph series I worked on years ago, one volume received numerous peer review comments that its chapters were long, disjointed, and didn't come together to tell a good story. There was no budget for what the reviewers recommended, which was a complete rewrite. Instead, we created a visual "roadmap" of the monograph, summarized each chapter relative to the overall goals of this roadmap, and created numerous sidebars highlighting key chapter issues in shaded boxes.

The end result? A volume that now flowed visually, allowed readers to "skim" the key points quickly, and was ultimately published with much better reviews.

Rule no. 6. Sum it up

Former Chrysler CEO Lee Iacocca once described his formula for a speech as follows: "I tell them what I'm going to tell them. Then I tell them. Then I tell them what I've told them."

This brings me to the third most common thing I edit in nonfiction projects: the summary-that-isn't-really-a-summary. You should close your project with a synthesis of what you have said, its significance for the reader, and possible future directions – and then ruthlessly delegate any further issues or tangential discussions to the body of the piece. In short, tell them what you have told them.

Rule no. 7. Packaging matters

You wouldn't show up for an important business meeting wearing gym shorts – in all likelihood, you would wear a nice suit or appropriate business clothes. In much the same way, the way you present your writing is often as important as the writing itself.

Once, my very first assignment for a new client was to create a report from a meeting. I could have simply created a word processing document with default formatting and summarized the meeting – and the client probably would have been fine with that.

Instead, however, I found a stylish document template and created a report with a cover, title page, right-indented paragraphs with "pull quotes" on the side highlighting the key points, and a nice use of greyscale colors throughout. It looked like it came from a million-dollar company. This made a huge impression on the client, who was profoundly grateful for making him look so good with his colleagues – and for me, it was the start of a six-figure relationship that spanned many years.

Templates abound, both within major word processing and desktop publishing programs and on the Internet. Many of them are free or available at very low cost. Whatever you use, a little up-front attention to the style of your content will almost always pay handsome dividends.

Pulling it all together

Now it's my turn to "tell you what I've told you." There is a real process behind making the leap from a good writer to a professional one, and you can summarize this process in a few simple steps:

- Create a killer opening.
- Use a clear introduction that frames your topic.
- Develop an outline that tells a clear story and guides your word count.
- Keep paragraphs and sections short.
- Break up your piece with figures, tables, bullets, and sidebars.
- Have a short summary that synthesizes the results of your work.
- Make it look professional.

I intentionally used the same process for this chapter, and guess what? Here you are reading it to the end! This is what I want for your own freelance writing work: to engage people, to teach them something new, and ultimately to help them – and you – benefit from the fruits of your writing.

CHAPTER 3

Secrets of Professional Ghostwriters

How would you like to have every book you write become a *New York Times* bestseller?

I can't promise you that. But I can suggest the next best thing – ghostwrite other people's books. Because first of all, it gives you the chance to write for some very successful people who may, indeed, hit the bestseller lists. But more important, the right kind of ghostwriting is lucrative enough that income-wise, it can be like writing a *New York Times* bestseller every time out of the starting gate.

Ghostwriting a book is much different from authoring one. For one thing, you don't have any rights to the words you create – your client does. Second, you must often work anonymously, frequently under non-disclosure agreements that would make your hair curl. And your creative freedom is generally very limited, because your job is to produce what the client wants you to write.

That said, it is one of the most satisfying and lucrative forms of freelance writing I have ever done. I have ghosted numerous books over the years, including a national top 100 business bestseller, the first book by the CEO of a multi-billion-dollar corporation, and several projects from leading figures in academia. I even did a children's book parody for a major New York firm.

(And if I told you any more about any of these projects, they would probably have to shoot me.)

Ghostwriting is a legitimate, accepted and ethical practice within the writing industry. Many well-known nonfiction books are actually written by ghostwriters, often on behalf of very successful people who use the skills of a good writer to get their message out quickly and professionally. A good ghost provides a valuable service for people who would otherwise be too busy to create their book, or know that they need the help of a professional. The underlying ideas, platform and message of the book normally rest with the client, but ghostwriters help these clients find their true voice.

As you succeed as a freelance writer and author, consider adding ghostwriting to your repertoire. The right kinds of ghostwriting projects can be substantial and pay very well. They can allow you to be a fly on the wall for a segment of society few people get to rub shoulders with. And the work is never boring.

Ghostwriting: the basics

First, let's start with the bad news: ghostwriting is a specialty field that is largely built on word-of-mouth. Unlike most professional freelance writing, where you can actively seek out clients and build a portfolio, ghostwriting involves developing a reputation as well as the right kinds of contacts.

And here is more bad news. For ghostwriting a book at professional-level rates, only the big fish can afford you. Think about what it would cost to hire a plumber or a contractor for the number of hours it takes to write a book, and you get the idea.

Then there is the good news: the right kind of ghostwriting projects can bring in tens of thousands of dollars, and some projects can even support a writer all year. It all depends on your clients, your target market, and the platform you build for yourself. So let's start with where to find these clients.

My advice is to aim your sights at very successful people. The ideal ghostwriting client is not your next-door neighbor who wants you to help him finish his novel, or the serial Kindle author who is looking for a cheap way to create the content for her next project. Ideal ghostwriting clients are people with public platforms, a good message, and professional responsibilities that make it difficult for them to write the book themselves – and are willing to pay a premium price for the right kind of help. These people include CEOs, professors, successful public speakers, media personalities, highly placed medical specialists, and other business and professional leaders.

So how do you tap this market? Not through direct sales and marketing efforts. Your chances of contacting a potential client at the exact moment they want to write a book is somewhere between slim and none. Instead, ghostwriting is more of a platform-building process. Here are my own personal strategies:

Build your experience. The primary thing that a ghost can offer a client is writing experience – and if at all possible, a publication track record. Personally, I started marketing myself as a ghost after having published several books under my own byline with major royalty publishers, as well as getting a local word-of-mouth ghostwriting project under my belt.

So what if you haven't published a book of your own yet? All is not lost. But your goal here is to convince clients that you can quickly and professionally write their book. Focus your portfolio-building efforts around projects for publishable markets, such as consumer or business articles, or projects where you take on the views and experiences of your clients and write engagingly about them.

Build your platform. How did people know to contact me for possible ghostwriting projects? I promoted myself as a ghostwriter on my website, including downloadable book excepts from my own books and bylined projects, and many of my early clients found me by Googling me.

Pro tip: Be sure to include your geographic information in your website. Many ghostwriting projects involve face-to-face meetings with clients, and in my case, my proximity to New York City was a major plus.

Get to know people in your target markets. I realize that you can't just go to a party tomorrow and introduce yourself to the CEO of a major television network. (Although if you can, definitely go!) But the road to good word-of-mouth as a writer is to meet people who have some connection to potential ghostwriting projects.

In my case, living in a college town, doing work for professors was a first step that led to my first ghostwriting project. Similarly, doing freelance writing projects for creative advertising and media firms helped me meet people in what is a surprisingly small and well-connected industry. As with all networking, your goal isn't to pester people for work — it is to delight in their company, get to know them, and give them a chance to learn about the great work you do. And it goes without saying, completely blow all of your clients away with good work and great service, because you never know where your next recommendation will come from.

Brand yourself. Know what sets you apart as a good ghost, and learn to be able to succinctly lead with that when you interview with potential clients.

Two particular hot buttons for clients are quality and speed. A ghostwriter is fundamentally a storyteller, and showing how you can turn a client's ideas into a good story helps your cause a great deal. And speed matters to most clients too. One of the most lucrative gigs I ever got came in a competitive interview where I felt I had no chance whatsoever — but when the client asked me if I could complete their book in four months, I said yes without hesitation. (And delivered.) It turned out everyone else that they interviewed said no, and the job was mine.

Sounding like a professional ghostwriter

So you've landed your first gig — perhaps a small local word-of-mouth project, or maybe your big break in a competitive interview process. Congratulations! Now what?

Before you start interviewing the client for their story and start writing, here are three first things I recommend doing to get your project off to a good start:

1. Provide a market analysis. I call this "the math lecture," because I break down currently successful books into their styles and formats, to help the client choose how their own book will read and flow. This important step helps your client position their book project against the market, and help you both decide how to structure the book.

For example, for business projects, I will deconstruct the current crop of bestsellers. I may point out that thought leaders like Seth Godin use dozens of micro-examples, and write bluntly and concisely in second person ("You need to be using Twitter. Now."). And that weighty tomes like James Surowiecki's *The Wisdom of Crowds* tend to use one or two credentialing examples per chapter, a strong opening hook, and fairly long paragraphs. And that a typical popular business book is written in third person with short paragraphs and lots of "eye candy" like charts, bullet items and sidebars. Then the client and I will discuss what they want their book to smell like in the marketplace. At times, I've even taken clients to bookstores to pull books off the shelf with me and look through them.

Remember that children's book parody I mentioned earlier? Even this project was the result of a similar process. As I studied other children's books and read about them, I got a feel for their format and style – including discovering that many children's books are written in a cadence known as anapestic meter (da-da DA DA, da-da-da-da DA DA). So what seemed at first glance like a very creative effort was actually a combination of rhyme and humor within a very specific format, and the result worked very well.

2. Deconstruct the client's voice. I look at a client's previous speeches, media appearances and articles, and create a "white paper" that breaks down how the client usually likes to communicate. I may note that the client tends to use simple declarative sentences, doesn't shy away from controversy, and reduces his arguments to simple analogies. I may also break down common themes such as the client's roots, home town or significant stories. Most clients are fascinated to see their personality and communications style reduced to a few sheets of paper, but once we reach consensus, this document then becomes my style guide for the book project. Never forget: your job as a ghostwriter is to sound like *them*, not you.

3. Create a detailed outline. At this point, you want to take the client's message and break it down into chapters, and then subheads within each chapter. As a rule of thumb, plan on about 500-1000 words per subhead and, for a typical business title, around 5000 words per chapter. (Although this could vary considerably, based on the market research you did in step 1.)

Once you have these three steps in place, you have a game plan for developing your client's book project — and then the heavy lifting of research, interviews and writing can begin in earnest.

Avoid the "five nevers"

There are also some important pitfalls to look out for when you are taking on a ghostwriting project. I call them the "five nevers." Here they are:

1. Never do a ghostwriting project in return for a share of the royalties. Ever! Books generally sell in frightfully small quantities, even for many successful books. In the vast majority of cases, you will never get compensated for more than a tiny fraction of the work you have put in, even at minimum-wage rates. The only time you should share in the work and royalties of a book project without further compensation is if you are a legitimate co-author, and the book itself benefits your career and platform.

Consider also that splitting royalties complicates the relationship with your client forever after, and can lead to hard feelings if it cuts into an already-small revenue stream for the client. And if you try to negotiate for a share of royalties, you are less competitive compared with other ghostwriters. My advice: unless you've been tapped to write the next Star Wars, stay away.

2. Never be a jerk about getting credit. I often tell clients, "The only credit I need on your book project is your signature on the check." Unless you are a highly experienced and in-demand ghostwriter, demanding to have your name on the cover makes you much less competitive versus other writers. Your goal is to get the gig, and build a good word-of-mouth reputation. Being a credit hog gets in the way of both of these goals.

So what about being able to share your work with other prospective clients? That is a separate negotiation from having your name on the project. I have often negotiated permission to show my work to other potential clients on a case-by-case basis. Also, I tell clients that if they like the job I have done for them, to feel free to mention me in the book's acknowledgements as an "editor." Either way, I always honor the client's wishes for anonymity.

Understand where you fit

To me, there is almost a spiritual aspect to why you shouldn't be a pain in the neck about things like royalties or credit: namely, it isn't really your book. In my humble opinion, books neither sell nor become successful because of your writing. They succeed because of the ideas and platform of the client. As I became a more experienced ghostwriter – and saw some clients land contracts and advances I could never dream of – it became clear to me that ghostwriters are really technicians, rather than the "author" of a client's book.

When people ask if I mind seeing a client's name on a book I wrote, my answer is always a resounding NO. I am always happy to serve anonymously as the humble scribe for people with great ideas. Ironically, most of my ghostwriting clients have actually been pretty good writers themselves. But they are busy running multi-billion-dollar companies, being academic superstars, or whatever, and don't have time to do the writing. So they call in a technician like me, much like they might call on a good plumber or contractor, and we're both happy.

3. Never work without a contract. I make it a point to be easy to work with. For some freelance writing projects, this means doing business on a handshake. (In over 20 years of freelancing, I have never been stiffed even a penny.) But ghostwriting projects have their own unique potential legal and liability issues. For example, what if you or the client decides to terminate your participation? What is expected from you in terms of confidentiality or non-disclosure? And what are the payment terms?

I will discuss two particularly important terms in the next two items, but in general, you need a contract for any ghostwriting project. The specifics of such contracts are beyond the scope of this book, but a quick online search of "ghostwriting contract" will yield a wealth of information ranging from tips to free or paid contract templates.

4. Never be liable for your client's content. More than any other form of writing, ghostwriting does carry the risk of being legally responsible for what your client asks you to write. You aren't likely to get sued for, say, writing a marketing brochure for a bank. But what if you ghostwrite a book about someone's quack medical ideas and someone's kid dies because of their advice, or someone feels slandered by what your client wrote about them? You could possibly be sued along with the client. So make sure you are legally protected up front, by establishing that the client's words are solely the client's responsibility.

The standard vehicle for this is a formal ghostwriting contract where the client indemnifies you against any legal issues with the resulting publication, including paying your attorney's expenses if necessary. Normally they should indemnify you for anything other than plagiarism (which is your responsibility). And in cases where the client will be publishing this book with a standard royalty publisher, make sure the contract specifies that you are included in the publisher's "errors and omissions" insurance covering against libel and other issues.

Finally, use your head when it comes to the content of the book, and don't be afraid to turn down work that doesn't feel right for you. If your client wants you to help him or her spout extreme political opinions, hate speech, dubious medical advice, or other legally contentious areas, it is often best to turn down the gig in the first place – and bonus points if you can point the client towards more socially acceptable or market-friendly ways to get their message out there.

5. Never charge by the project. I've saved the best one for last. Because it flies in the face of most published advice about ghostwriting projects. ALWAYS charge by the hour. NEVER charge by the project. Trust me on this one – you AND the client will be much happier if you charge on a time and materials basis, by the hour, for any writing you do.

Here's why: it takes away the biggest source of conflict and disagreement between a ghostwriter and his or her client. It makes gigs much more possible in the first place. And often, it actually turns out to be more lucrative.

Estimating an accurate cost for a ghostwriting project is like trying to predict the weather a month from now. Even for a first draft. You probably know how quickly you write, of course. But you don't always know how much research will be required, how much detail the client wants, and above all, how much clients will change their mind as the project proceeds. And any major change has the potential to create a tug-of-war about project scope and costs. Writing someone's book is like a marriage in every good and bad sense of the word, and you have to be prepared for surprises along the way.

Conversely, charging by the hour is your key to saying "yes" to everything the client wants. When I first meet with a client, I tell them, "My rate is $X per hour. You are welcome to use me for three hours or three years if you wish. (Note: Clients never use you for just three hours.) I don't mind if you bring in other writers, write part of it yourself, or even change your mind every week. This is *your* book, and I will always be at your service."

For one major ghostwriting project, involving a large corporation and multiple stakeholders, my earnings for revisions and reviews turned out to be nearly as much as the actual writing of the book. For another, working by the hour allowed a client with a tight budget to have me help her with specific chapters and get her book to the publisher on schedule. And for others, it completely took away the "writers ego" problem of working with multiple contributors.

Some people will tell you that charging by the project is the key to creating a high-value quote that is more lucrative than charging by the hour. But trust me on this one – this advantage rings hollow when a client expects major last-minute rewrites, constantly changes his mind, or picks at everything you write. Or you don't get the gig in the first place because your price was too high. Horror stories about ghostwriting projects gone bad are sadly all too common. By having a fair hourly rate, and putting the client in control of his or her own budget, you'll smile no matter what the client wants, and work together as a team.

Ghostwriting can be rarified and lucrative territory for a freelance writer. It is not for the beginner, and it is truly an art form unto itself. But for those who follow the largely unspoken rules of this craft and build a platform for themselves, it is often a very satisfying way to make good money writing. I personally never get tired of seeing books that I helped write for others on the shelves of major bookstores, and appreciate the opportunity to be a midwife for the ideas of some very talented and successful people.

CHAPTER 4

Marketing Your Services

f you dropped me off tomorrow, flat broke, in a strange city, I honestly believe that within six months I would still have a productive, upper-middle-class career as a freelance writer. Why? Because I have a process that works for marketing my services. And you will too, if you follow the same steps.

Here is a summary of the process I have used for years:

- Target your market
- Create a portfolio
- Knock on doors
- Grow your word-of-mouth
- Build your network

When people think of the word "marketing," they often think about the first three steps. That's good – at first, there is no substitute for a traditional sales effort in building your practice. But it is actually the last two steps that form the bedrock of a lasting career as a writer.

You see, your goal is not to land a gig – it is to land customers. Because gigs come and go, but customers often last a long time. I am still writing away for people I worked with 10, 15, even 20 years ago. And it would not be an exaggeration to say that once I built a strong enough base of regular customers, my marketing strategy often consisted of simply waiting for the phone to ring. That is where you eventually want to get to in your own freelance writing business.

Step 1: Target your market

What is the very worst market for a freelance writer? "Everyone."

Niches matter. When you have a niche, several good things happen. Prospects and potential customers pay attention to you. Your work commands a premium. You get more referral and word-of-mouth business. And it adds a laser focus to the skills and portfolio you develop.

So how do you choose a niche? Start with the market in your area, and the expertise you bring to the table. For example:

- If you live in a community with several manufacturing firms, consider writing manuals or marketing materials geared towards these industries.
- The pharmaceutical industry is clustered in specific areas of the country, and has specialized requirements for both its production and promotional writing needs.
- For me personally, living in a small college town with two major universities, academic writing and editing became my ticket to more clients and writing projects.
- If you live in Los Angeles, the entertainment industry is a big source of potential clients. (And not just press releases for movie stars – there is a whole industry of support firms that need manuals, blogs, press releases, marketing literature and more.) If you live in New York City, the advertising industry has a ceaseless need for creative copy. In Seattle, technology firms dominate. And so on.

No one says that you are limited to just one niche. I certainly wasn't. At any given time, my portfolio of products spanned several fields – technical writing, copywriting, ghostwriting, editing, and much more. The important thing about choosing a niche is to create unique expertise to show clients. Now, let's look at the specifics of doing that.

Step 2: Create a portfolio

Your potential clients really only have one concern when you meet with them (besides whether you ate too many onions for lunch): can you deliver what they need? And there is one time-honored way to demonstrate this to them: *your portfolio*.

When it comes to your portfolio, writers have one huge advantage over nearly any other profession: we have a great deal of control over our credentials. And we can even create these credentials out of thin air if we need to.

Think about it. If you want to be a doctor, you had better have a degree from medical school. If you want to be a successful architect, you generally need to have a few buildings under your belt. If you want to be a movie producer, you need access to expensive cameras and editing tools. For that matter, if you want to pump people's septic tanks, you need invest in heavy equipment. But you can start down the road to getting hired as a freelance writer – this month, if you wish – by simply creating high-quality samples of your own writing. And you can even create them yourself, before you get a single paying client.

But first, there is a right way and a wrong way to create a portfolio:

The Right Way: Put together a purpose-written, curated collection of writing samples that show your writing expertise for the markets you want to get hired in.

The Wrong Way: Pull together every scrap of writing you have ever done since high school, whether it is commercially viable or not, and tie it together with a big piece of string.

Obviously, if you have experience writing in the genre of your potential clients, you will want to feature these pieces in your portfolio. Bring your "A" game and choose your very best work, of course – quality counts much, much more than quantity here. Favor pieces that are easy to read, are colorful, or were written for major markets like larger companies where possible.

Pro tip: If you are a published author – particularly a royalty-published author – your own books are a great calling card as part of your portfolio. We will talk more about book publishing in the next section. Meanwhile, understand that publishing credentials often move you to the head of the line with prospective clients – so hand out copies of your books like candy when you are prospecting.

But what if your experience base in your target market is a little thin? It is always a conundrum that you need experience to get hired, and you need to get hired to get experience. If possible, supplement your portfolio with closely related pieces: for example, if you are trying to write documentation for a manufacturing company, you might include a sample of a manual for a consumer product.

Finally, what if you have NO prior experience or publications in your target market? Here are some creative strategies you might use:

- Select pieces that show off your general writing skills, and be prepared to draw parallels between these pieces and your clients' needs.
- Develop custom samples of materials aimed at the client's market. For example, for a marketing agency, create some brochure or web copy, or a sample advertisement.
- Depending on the client, you might even consider showing specific improvements to their existing materials. For example, I once contacted an Asian electronics manufacturer – but not before downloading one of their manuals, which was poorly written and translated, and completely rewriting it in flawless English. This overture soon opened the door to a competitive bid to do more work for them.

Next comes the packaging of your portfolio. Should it be in hardcopy form or posted online? The answer is yes – do both. The former will serve as your talking points in live meetings with prospective clients, while the latter makes it possible to share links to your material via email or social media. Either way, sweat the details of packaging this material – use a high-quality binder or folio and logo for your hardcopies, and an eye-catching website template for your online materials. Be sure to have your business card or contact information clearly visible with both kinds of packages, to make it as easy as possible for clients to follow up with you.

Pro tip: Cloud storage services such as Box (www.box.com) or Microsoft OneDrive are often easy, cost-free ways to store documents online for links to your portfolio materials. If you do not have a high volume of customer downloads, storage space on your own website may be a viable option as well.

The goal of your proposal is twofold: show your competency as a writer, and make your freelance writing practice look like a million bucks. And don't be afraid to have multiple portfolios for multiple markets. In this profession, preparation and targeting count for everything.

Step 3: Knock on doors

This is where the rubber meets the road: getting your work in front of potential clients. If you have done a good enough job of targeting your market, you should have a clear, specific list of organizations on your list to contact. And if you have paid close attention to finding "boring" markets with less competition and ongoing needs, you will have a much better chance of getting your foot in the door.

Here are some specific tips for making the most of the prospecting process:

Size up your prospects. What is your ideal market, as a beginning freelancer? In my experience, organizations with between 200 and 800 employees – in visual terms, the kind of companies you would find in an average business park. Why is this? Companies with between 200 and 800 employees are large enough to have needs for ongoing written content – and small enough that they may not have an in-house department for producing it, or need to supplement this staff for peak periods. Moreover, small-to-medium businesses like these are less likely to have onerous procurement processes for hiring freelancers.

Of course, you need not limit your search to businesses or organizations of this size. You may find plenty of lucrative work with a two-person startup company, a small non-profit agency, or a major company with tens of thousands of employees. And of course, you should follow the markets that need your expertise, whatever their size. But small-to-medium sized ongoing businesses are often a great place to start prospecting.

Get names. You are never selling to organizations – you are selling to people. So always get names of potential hiring authorities. These would include job titles such as director of marketing, head of technical documentation, manager of publications, and the like. For smaller organizations, you may be speaking with senior management directly. In general, it is best to aim too high than too low in your search, because senior people are likely to refer you to the right people – perhaps with their recommendation.

How do you obtain these names? In some cases, through online research, using search engines and/or professional directories such as LinkedIn. In other cases, through your own network of contacts – often someone knows someone who knows someone. And if all else fails, ask! There is generally no harm in calling people at an organization to get the names of appropriate contacts, as long as you are polite and professional about it. Just remember that traditional "gatekeepers" such as a company's human resources department are much less likely to disclose specific names than directly involved employees or managers.

Get face-to-face. There is honestly no substitute for meeting prospective clients face-to-face. If I had a choice between sending 100 emails versus having five meetings with prospects, I would take the meetings in a heartbeat. When people meet with you, they get to know you, remember you and your portfolio, and are much more likely to do business with you. Plus, you get to hear and respond to their needs, and customize your pitch around these needs.

Make your pitch. Here is a simple process I use for trying to arrange meetings with prospective clients: send an email introducing myself and requesting an informational meeting, follow up by phone if necessary, and then move forward with people who are interested. I also ask friends, colleagues and contacts to make a warm introduction to people who might be interested in hiring a writer. Here is a sample of a good prospecting email:

Dear Sandra,

My name is Rich Gallagher, and I am a freelance writer and former software developer with extensive experience in writing and editing software documentation.

Whether you have ongoing needs for manuals or support content, or "crunch periods" where you need outside help to meet your release deadlines, I am available any time on demand. I work quickly, with a minimum of demands on your product development team, and never, ever miss a deadline.

I would love to meet briefly with you, just to introduce myself and drop off some sample materials. I will call you later this week to see if you would like to have a short meeting. Thanks!

Best, Rich

My pitch is simple, benefit-driven, and designed to quickly assess whether this prospect needs the kinds of services I have to offer – now, or in the future. If they agree to meet with me, great! And if they don't? Also great! I have no interest in bothering people who don't want or need what I have to offer, so off the list they go.

My secret sales weapon

I have a secret. A secret that helps me close more sales than just about anyone I know. In fact, it not only helps me close more sales, it almost magically turns prospects into long-term client relationships. I have been using it successfully for years and years. Ready to hear my secret? Here you go:

I honestly couldn't give a rat's patootie whether I make the sale or not.

That's it. Nothing more. This one principle guides everything I say and do, with prospects and customers alike. Here is how it changes everything:

• When someone asks who is the best writer for them, most of you will say "me," even under pain of torture. I will frankly discuss the pros and cons of what I and others do best.

• When prospects tell you they need more time, you will try to rush them into acting now. I won't, because I don't care.

• When people decide to go with another provider, you will do everything you can to salvage the sale. And probably annoy the bejeebers out of them. Meanwhile, I will shake their hand and sleep soundly knowing that they have my coordinates if they need anything.

Mind you, I love being successful. But I made a decision many years ago to take the tactics of every pushy, annoying, hi-I'm-just-calling-to-check-in-with-you salesperson I knew, and do exactly the opposite. And when I found out how spectacularly well it worked, I kept doing it. Which, in large part, explains why I live a very nice life with so many good client relationships.

Now, of course, there are things I care very much about. Like my credibility. Or keeping a client happy. Or working hard at being very, very good at what I do. But when it comes to making the sale, I have more in common with the 17-year-old slacker with his baseball cap on backwards than with most professional salespeople.

I refer to my marketing approach as "wheeling out the dessert cart" – when I am face to face with a prospect I get to know them, listen to what they need, and share what I can do to help them, with no sales pressure whatsoever. I find that when your primary goal is to simply delight in the company of your prospects, and your secondary goal is to share your portfolio and experience, the decision to hire you – now, or later – becomes much easier.

Step 4. Grow your word-of-mouth

You might think that for the rest of your freelancing career, prospecting will be the most important part of building your business, right? WRONG.

At least in my markets, good writers are rare and hard to find. And I only really had to prospect early in my consulting career. Frankly, for most of the past 20 years, the vast majority of my business has come from word-of-mouth from satisfied clients. And my marketing approach has often involved nothing more than waiting for the phone to ring. So what I am going to say next is the single most important thing you will learn about marketing your practice:

When I get a writing gig, particularly from a brand-new client, my job isn't just to write for them. Or just to do a good job. *It is to completely blow them away with the quality, speed and courtesy of working with me.*

Let's break this down into specifics:

- Your job isn't to meet deadlines – it is to beat them, with gusto
- Your job isn't to produce good writing – your job is to make your client look awesome

- Your job isn't to do a good layout – it is to take their materials to another level
- Your job isn't to not cause problems – it is to be an absolute pleasure to work with
- Your job isn't to set limits with clients – when they ask you to jump, ask "how high?"

In other words, the answer is always "yes." Here is my strategy: get up at 5 AM to go to an out-of-town client meeting? No problem. Stay up until 5 AM to meet a rush deadline? You got it. Accommodate the client's umpteenth change of mind? Absolutely, my pleasure. My being a little crazy about good service has made a HUGE difference in people recommending and hiring me.

This same principle applies to all the predictable frustrations that come with being self employed. I call it the PITA principle – which is an acronym for being a Pain In The Anatomy. I work really hard to NOT be a PITA with all of my clients. Take getting paid. Normally, most invoices should get paid within 30 days. Some clients might be a few days or even a few weeks late paying. Should I get paid on time? Of course I should. But if I am bugging a client's accounts payable department on day 31 after my invoice, I am being a pain in the anatomy. So I have a long fuse, I am willing to wait a reasonable amount of time for clients to get their act together, and I am always unfailingly polite with a client's financial people.

All sorts of things can and will go wrong with client projects. They can get delayed, funding can get held up, or specifications may change. Different people in a client's organization may give you conflicting instructions or even hate each other. Sometimes projects even get cancelled. No matter what, my goal is the same: never, ever be a PITA. Because you know what? If you knew how much business I've done over the years with clients who stuck with me because I wasn't a PITA when things went wrong, you would be exactly the same way.

Slow-paying clients can be your best friends

At one point during a major project – representing a large portion of my income that year – I hadn't been paid in six months, AND had to foot my own travel bill for a client meeting in Chicago. How did I feel at this point?

I felt fantastic! Why? Because this was an extremely lucrative project, and because I was able to ride the peculiar waves of its cash flow, it was MINE. And I eventually got paid for every penny of my time and expenses. It was funded through periodic contract appropriations that sometimes took a long period of time to get approved, and I was more than happy to wait these slow times out.

The lesson here? Slow-pay clients - not ones who are short of cash, but rather ones with lots of bureaucracy in their payment process – can be your best friend. Because most people can't afford to play in these situations, and if you can, you often have a lucrative market all to yourself.

Step 5. Grow your network

This is the single biggest reason I am successful, and the single biggest reason you will be successful: the network of people who know me and like me. This network includes not only clients and their employees, but fellow writers and entrepreneurs, professional organizations, and other contacts.

Clearly, you are creating opportunities for yourself when you contact potential clients. What you don't realize is that you are also creating opportunities when you socialize with other writers, help other colleagues make connections, speak to professional groups, or get to know people at conferences.

Understand that your goal in networking isn't to land work. It is to get to know people and delight in each other's company. And from there, let these relationships serve you in the future. Here are some examples of how these connections have served me:

- A local entrepreneur who I met at a networking group hooked me up with a $25,000 project (and earned a nice finder's fee for it)
- I shared an advance draft of one of my first books with a related industry organization. One of the people who worked for their director later started her own company, and we have done thousands of dollars per year of business ever since.
- After giving a talk at a local university, the professor who hosted me asked me to develop an orientation program for her graduate students – and we have now been teaching it together for nearly a decade.

But here is the important part: I enjoyed getting to know each of these people, and had no idea when I met any of them that I would ever do business with them. And there were many other people I have met and like who have never crossed my palms with silver. But my successful freelance writing career literally stands on the shoulders of a large community of people whom I now consider my friends.

Also, realize that connection goes both ways – for example, as I started cutting back my own practice and transitioned to retirement recently, I referred a lucrative client relationship to two other fellow writers. One of them I knew, and the other was recommended to me by another (busy) writer I knew and trusted. Which is perhaps the most important point of all about networking: it works best when you have an attitude of being of service to others. And often the more you give, the more you get.

Love your competitors

One category of networking deserves special mention: fellow freelance writers. Get to know them, cheer on their successes, and help them out whenever you can. Why? For three important reasons:

- *When a writer is too busy to take on a gig him or herself, who do you think they will send it to? To people they know and like, of course.*

- *Good writers are always learning and growing in their profession, so keeping up with other writers is a good way to keep abreast of the market and compare notes about your craft.*

- *Writing is often a solitary craft. It is good for your mental health, and your social life, to keep the company of other people who understand your profession and your life.*

From zero to 60 (thousand)

Now, let's talk frankly about getting started. The hardest part of any freelance writing career is the startup. Why? Because (a) it takes time to build an initial pipeline of clients, and (b) for most people, especially when they live paycheck to paycheck, it is hard to make the flying leap to self-employment.

But that doesn't mean that freelancing isn't secure. Quite the contrary: to me, having a single job that can get whacked at any time seems risky and crazy, while having a stable of clients and gigs is sober and rational. If you lose your job, it can be a disaster – but if you lose one of many gigs or clients (as you will sometimes), big whoop. So here are some creative ways to help make the leap to a more secure lifestyle:

Become a temp. Temporary help agencies can be a real boon to getting your business off the ground, and they were a huge help to me personally when I got started. They don't always pay well, and there are rules in place that sometimes make it hard to work directly for their clients later. But writing is a fertile ground for temporary assignments, because they tend to come in waves for any organization – for example, a new product gets released, and now they need the manuals for it. Many major organizations turn to temp agencies in situations like this because it is one-stop shopping for them – which means they often need writers quickly, which lowers the bar to get your foot in the door. If you are just getting started, temp agencies can really be your best friend.

Have multiple streams of income. The great thing about being a consultant is that you can do whatever you wish, with no loss of status. Write? You're a consultant. Train people? You're a consultant. Mow people's lawns? By golly, you are still a consultant. So think about some of the things you might do *and* be a writer – anything from other demand services to a part-time job.

Consider customer funding. For your first projects, consider offering your customers a discounted retainer arrangement – they agree to pay you a minimum amount per month, in exchange for a lower hourly rate and/or guaranteed availability. Alternatively, you could also focus your attention on writing gigs that involve long-term contracts, such as government or organizational projects.

Save your money. Finally, one of the more important ways to prepare for a freelance career is to save as much of a cash cushion as you can before you take the leap. This cash cushion gives you the time to get your business off the ground. Even more important, it can take away some of the emotional pressures that can hurt your business, like taking gigs that aren't right for you, or appearing desperate for work or payment in front of clients (which is a big no-no). I personally recommend putting aside six months of living expenses if possible before you take the leap.

I can see some of you rolling your eyes already, especially if you live paycheck to paycheck. Does saving this kind of sum seem like an impossible wall to climb? Not so fast. You may have an initial gig that eases the amount you need at first. Or assets you can sell. Or expenses that can be cut back. Some people refinance their homes, and later pay themselves back. (I do, however, recommend that you avoid raiding your retirement savings, because of the effect it would have on its long-term growth.) Whatever you do, think creatively about putting aside a cushion to help your business start, and eventually grow.

These strategies in this chapter will also serve you well if your pipeline starts to run dry. Consider temp work, build connections, broaden your geographic net or scope of potential clients if needed, and never forget to target "boring" markets that are lucrative and relatively easy to enter. And don't forget the basics: be sure to get trusted feedback about whether you need to step up your game and write better.

The main takeaway from this chapter is that freelance writing is – more than anything – a business built on relationships. Writing clients tend to have ongoing needs, hang on to good writers, and recommend them to their colleagues. This makes it an ideal career for people who hate to sell! And a secure living for people who can build good client relationships, take great care of their clients, and above all bring their "A" game to their writing. With the right marketing strategy, you too can build a successful practice and take your place in the fraternity of successful freelance writers.

The One Big Secret of Book Publishing

So you want to write a book. And sell it to a major royalty publisher. Great!

First, the bad news. Writing and publishing books is not, in and of itself, a road to riches for most writers. We'll explore this in more detail a little later. For now, here is my own example: I am about as published as they come, with nine books from major royalty publishers since 1994, and gross sales of over a million dollars. My body of work includes two major category bestsellers, several books with foreign or audio editions, and four book club selections. But in my best years, I have probably earned little more than a minimum wage income from writing my own books.

So why bother including a section of landing a publishing contract as part of *The Million Dollar Writer*? Because, quite simply, publishing a legitimate royalty published book is the fastest way to supercharge your income as a freelancer.

- First, it gives you instant credibility with clients. It puts you at the top of the credentials list compared with people who have never published a book, or have only self-published.

- Second, it opens the door to a wide range of high-income opportunities such as public speaking and ghostwriting, which we will discuss in a later chapter. I've even had lucrative gigs developing courses about my books for my own publisher.
- Finally, even though books are rarely major sources of income, they do pay. Over the course of my writing career, I have earned a six-figure sum from book royalties and advances, and I still regularly get four-figure checks every year from ongoing royalties for my own books.

Book writing for royalty publishers is analogous to rock musicians recording for a major label. In many if not most cases, the royalties from the actual sales of the record generally doesn't represent a real livelihood. But hit records, even minor ones, open the door to a lucrative, lifelong stream of income from sources such as touring, clinics, and other areas. And that alone makes it a worthwhile quest. This is why you, too, should be trying to publish your work with the literary equivalent of a "major label."

Which leads me to the primary purpose for this section. I honestly do not believe that placing a book with a royalty publisher is like winning the lottery. Thousands of people do it each and every year, and most of them aren't famous. And I truly believe that with the right guidance and technique, any good writer can join the club. So let's start with what I believe is the real secret to publishing a book.

The secret of royalty publishing

Be aware that for nonfiction books, your goal isn't to write a book. It is to write a book *proposal* – a 30-50 page summary of your book project, with a summary pitch, outline, competitive analysis, marketing plan, and sample chapters. Publishers then decide, based on the strength of this proposal, whether to offer you a contract to actually write the book.

We will cover the mechanics of a good proposal in a subsequent chapter. But for now, the good news is that your next book contract may be as little as 30 pages away. With the caveat that your success as a nonfiction author now rests on the strength of your *ideas*, not your turgid prose.

There are lots of variables in whether a book proposal gets accepted or not. But the single biggest factor in the success of your proposal has little to do with how well you write, whether you compose a good query, or how neatly you prepare your proposal. This factor is simple, and obvious. And it will be the very first question an agent or publisher will ask about your proposal: *Will it sell?*

Which leads me to what I truly feel is the one big secret of book publishing – the one that almost always determines whether you succeed or not. Here it is:

Work backwards from the market. Not forward from your crazy idea.

Now, listen carefully. I am not suggesting that you shouldn't decide what you want to write about. And I would never ever suggest that you ignore your interests and expertise simply to follow what is popular. What I am saying, however, is that people who make a *market-informed* decision about what to write about stand a much better chance of landing a book contract with a major royalty publisher.

Here is an example of a conversation I have often had with budding book writers. He tells me he wants to find a publisher for his nautical memoir *Three Sheets to the Wind*. I suggest that I am not aware of a market for nautical memoirs. He responds by furrowing his brow and saying, "This is why I need to write this book! I'll have the whole market to myself!" At which point I politely excuse myself and start looking for a pole to bang my head against.

Or the fledgling entrepreneur who has spent all her career as an entomology professor, and now wants to create a book entitled *What Bugs Can Teach You about Success*. She stares blankly at me as I suggest the possibility of cutting her teeth on more popular book topics, and can't stop railing about why the local TEDx conference rejected her proposal.

I have frankly been guilty of this as well. Over a decade ago, I had a moderately successful book from a major publisher entitled *The Soul of an*

Organization. My fantasy was that I would go around the country helping organizations uncover the core values of success. I soon discovered the hard way that no one wanted to find the soul of their organization, but nearly everyone needed customer service and communications skills training – and the rest is history.

Nowadays, nearly all my books and training programs are specifically purpose-written around a clear market with existing competition. As a result, I spare myself the burden of trying to convince people that they need what I am offering. Instead, all I have to do is be really, really good.

This principle of following the market applies for any creative endeavor serving the public, including speaking, writing, and even performing. Here are some examples from each of these areas showing how people eventually learned to wrap their interests around the market:

- One dog training expert tried repeatedly to hold workshops on – to be obvious – training your dog. And couldn't get arrested. But when she changed her topic to how to prevent dog attacks, suddenly every postal worker and delivery service employee was interested, and she had a booming business.
- There are hundreds of marginally successful books on delegating work tasks. But when author Tim Ferriss decided to title his book *The Four-Hour Work Week*, he struck gold.
- One of my engineering classmates from Cornell, whom I've never met, used to juggle his technical career with an off-hours gig as a local sketch comedy performer. Later he learned to combine these two interests in a way that fit children's television, and what happened? He became Bill Nye the Science Guy.

Now let's focus on books, with a personal example. As a successful manager, I wanted to write a book for years on how to coach people. But this was a crowded market with a lot of existing bestselling books. So I knew that simply writing "How To Coach People by Rich Gallagher" would probably be a waste of time. Instead, I looked at what the market needed – an evidence-based strategy for handling difficult conversations with people at work. There had been a string of bestsellers in recent years on this subject, but few had a "system" with its roots in published behavioral science.

So one year, during my graduate work as a psychotherapist, one of my courses discussed strength-based therapy – the radical concept that negotiations go much better when you speak to other people's strengths and interests, rather than trying to convince them that you are right and they are wrong. I took this principle, together with my own life experiences, and wrote a book proposal that applied it to really tough workplace situations – like toxic bosses and employees who constantly come in late.

The result was my best selling book ever, *How to Tell Anyone Anything*. It landed a book contract on the strength of good competitive analysis that compared my research-based approach to current bestsellers, and eventually landed on the shelf of every major bookstore in America (even becoming a bargain book!). It was published in multiple languages, and is still in print nearly a decade later. (And as an added benefit, the royalties and speaking fees from this book ended up paying for much of my graduate school!)

Another example was my book *What to Say to a Porcupine*, a worldwide customer service and business humor bestseller that was a finalist for 800-CEO-READ's Business Book of the Year in 2008. My strategy? After observing the hot success of the "business fable" genre of short, easy-to-read fictional books teaching business lessons, I decided to go back to their source: Aesop's fables. I meticulously researched the format and history of these fables, and faithfully crafted a book around its format – 500 words per fable, stories that alternated between animals and people as protagonists, and of a course a moral. The resulting product was a big hit because it was a great market fit.

(And in the interests of full disclosure, I later wrote what I felt was an equally good follow-up fable entitled *The Last Customer*, a story about what happened when a business decided to treat every customer like their last customer. Unfortunately I got busy with other projects, and by the time I was ready to submit it, the business fable genre was deader than a doornail. It sits on my hard drive to this day.)

Putting the secret to work

The one common denominator between most successful book projects I am aware of is that they started with *market-informed* proposals that leveraged books and genres that were already selling successfully. Then they offered something that added value to these markets.

So how do you create a book proposal that is based on a well-researched market? First and foremost, there is one thing I do differently than almost any wannabe writer I know, and it is the single biggest reason I am successful: I **study the genre** I am writing in. Go to a bookstore sometime, and you will see most people browsing through books. Watch me and you'll see me pulling one book after another off the shelf, running my finger along the pages, muttering to myself, and occasionally even pulling out a calculator. (Did I tell you I have an engineering degree?) While others read books, I deconstruct them. And when I finally sit down to write, it is a thoughtfully composed performance informed by the style of what sells.

Studying the genre is NOT the same as copying another person's style. I have my own style, thank you. In fact, I have lots of them, having published in genres that include popular business books, social science, and even fictional stories. Rather, I have a good, general sense of the audience I am writing for. Here are some examples of what I look for:

Titles: Your title is at least twice as important as your content. Really. Think about it - what made you pull a book off the shelf or on Amazon? More important, if you had a choice between titling the same book *Finding Good Business Partners and Suppliers* or *The Four-Hour Work Week*, which one would sell better? Tim Ferriss certainly figured that one out! Sweat the title first, and make it "smell" like other successful books in your genre.

Opening hook: Open any unsuccessful self-published book at random, and I'll bet it just starts right in talking about the topic of the book. By comparison, successful royalty published books tend to hook the reader with a good story, an "a-ha" moment, or a credentialing example.

There are a small number of very specific types of opening hooks for popular non-fiction business books, including personal narratives, credentialing examples, and emotional connections. Study them all and then think of them as clubs in your golf bag, ready to thoughtfully choose to fit your project.

Word count: When I wrote business fables, these projects never topped 25,000 words, used short paragraphs, and were built around simple ideas. If I write a thick book with lots of jargon, no matter how funny or well-written I make it, I couldn't have played in this market. Similarly, my business self-help books generally tipped the scales at 50-70,000 words, had clear reader benefits in each chapter, were written in third person, and used lots of "eye candy" such as sidebars and examples to break up a wall of prose.

Note also that books – and attention spans – have been steadily getting shorter in this Internet era of information on demand. My first book for AMACOM, a major business publisher, weighed in at a little over 80,000 words. But by the time I developed my fourth book for them, eight years later, I had a strict upper limit of 45,000 words. Pay attention to length and wordcount trends in the genres you are writing in, particularly for recently published books.

Paragraph length and style: Lots of choices here. Do you want to write a weighty tome like James Surowiecki's *The Wisdom of Crowds*, a thought leadership book like Malcolm Gladwell's *The Tipping Point*, or a quick read like Seth Godin's *Tribes*? Surowiecki runs out his anecdotes over several pages, Gladwell hooks your attention with thought-provoking ideas at the beginning of each chapter, and Godin uses lots of short, punchy examples. Each of them "smell" the way they do because of reproducible points of style.

So go out there and break down your favorite books. Study their opening hooks, their paragraph lengths, their chapter structures, and the way they keep your interest flowing. Think of how these things might affect your own unique writing voice, and how you want your own books to be seen. Then get writing!

Some of you may be saying, "But what about people who succeed with totally original ideas?" Fair enough. Here is what I might suggest: take everyone you know personally who has done this, compare them against the number of people you know who have been struck by lightning or won the lottery, and then decide whether to follow your bliss or not.

Ideas are a dime a dozen. Markets are precious and often surprisingly hard to build from scratch. Start with the market first, and you will make your path to success that much easier.

CHAPTER 6

Aspire to Royalty

Debates have raged for years about royalty-published books – where a publisher pays you to write a book, and shoulders the full cost of publication and distribution – versus self-publishing. There are valid arguments on both sides of this issue. Especially nowadays, where the cost of self-publishing a book for markets like Amazon.com can be next to nothing.

If your goal is to sell a million dollars of books, however, the debate is over for many people: royalty publishing is the way to go.

The case for royalty publishing

If you are trying to build a platform as a successful writer, I strongly recommend you write at least one traditional, royalty published book – or at the very least, a book whose quality would attract a traditional publisher. Here are just a few of the reasons why:

1. It forces your book to be good. When you listen to music, do you usually listen to unsigned bands, or to artists who have signed with a major recording label? Most of you will say the latter. And for many people, it is exactly the same way with books.

If you don't believe me, try an experiment some time. Go on a website like Amazon.com, where you can look at previews of book content online, and look at the bestselling royalty-published books in a given genre. Then look at self-published books in the same genre. Notice a difference in their quality? And in their sales rankings?

There is a reason many self-published books have a hard time getting shelf space at bookstores, or getting featured in mass-market media: they haven't passed the ultimate test of quality, namely whether someone else will pay to publish it. So even if it ultimately makes more economic sense to you to self-publish your book, you should at least set a goal of being *good enough* to be royalty-published.

2. Wider distribution. Today, anyone can literally sit down at their personal computer and have a book available on Amazon.com *this week*. So why should they bother going the traditional publishing route? Because their book will be visible in a lot more places where people look for books. Traditional bookstores, airports, and even prime search results on Amazon.com are largely the domain of books that sell in large quantities, which in turn still mostly come from paying publishers.

3. Higher average sales. Most self-published authors do not earn enough on their books to make a single car payment. Says who? Um, self-published authors themselves. In a survey of over 1000 of them, The Guardian reported in 2012 that over half of them make less than $500 per year[2]. And many of the more successful ones publish fiction, which is often more friendly to developing an organic market online.

By comparison, the average royalty advance for first-time authors is reported by at least one knowledgeable source as being in the $10,000 range[3]. Yes, some self-published books do sell in large quantities, and

---

[2] Flood, Alison, "Stop the press: half of self-published authors earn less than $500," The Guardian, May 24, 2012, https://www.theguardian.com/books/2012/may/24/self-published-author-earnings

[3] Kozlowski, Michael, "First Time Authors Normally Get a $10,000 Advance from a Major Publishing Company," GoodEReader.com, January 16, 2014,

traditionally-published ones can and do crash and burn. But since the latter generally average per-copy royalties of a buck or two, the math indicates that the average royalty-published book sells thousands of copies.

4. The Fourth Estate. In general, it is extremely rare for a self-published author to get the attention of major media outlets. Again, for the same reason most people don't listen to unsigned bands – a perceived quality gap that keeps many authors on the other side of that glass wall. There are exceptions, of course, but the quest to build a media platform around your book gets a lot harder without a publisher.

With a good traditionally-published book, media outlets often approach you. For example, when a customer service scandal broke and went viral a few years ago, I got a phone call the next day from *Time Magazine* – and 700 words later, my take on the situation was in print the very same afternoon. Over time my own books have been featured in media channels such as AOL, MSN, *BusinessWeek*, CNN, major newspapers and morning drive radio – and all of these markets came to me, not the other way around. This, in turn, substantially helped build my platform as an author and speaker: for example, a feature in the *Toronto Globe and Mail* boosted one of my books to become one of Canada's top 250 books on Amazon.

5. Platform credibility. Even a single traditionally-published book legitimately confers the title of "published author" on you. This, in turn, can become a credential for a great deal of ancillary revenue-generating activities including speaking, coaching, teaching workshops, and other areas. We will discuss these in a later chapter.

The impact of a successful book on my own platform was dramatic. After one of my books hit number 1 in a couple of major business categories, I was literally on an airplane every week for two months straight delivering keynote speeches all over the United States. That year I went from speaking

---

http://goodereader.com/blog/indie-author-news/first-time-authors-normally-get-a-10000-advance-from-a-major-publishing-company

a dozen or so times per years to 40-50 dates per year, and continued at that pace for many years afterward.

Proponents of self-publishing do have some arguments in their favor, which we will explore next. But ultimately, the decision to seek a publisher or not boils down to a question of percentages. How likely is your book to sell in large quantities on your own, versus under the wing of a publisher? For most people, in most circumstances, the numbers lean in favor of traditional publishing.

Another view of self-publishing: books versus businesses

Some people do, in fact, make a very good living through the sales of their own self-published books or other information products. In my experience, the majority of them have the following things in common:

- *These products often revolve around self-help and financial success: for example, how to become self-employed, sell information products, become a coach, etc.*

- *They are not just - or often even primarily - book authors. They are first and foremost running an online business.*

- *A great deal of their efforts revolve around things like list building, creating an effective sales funnel, affiliate marketing, and all the other skills that come with being an online marketer*

Others build niche business efforts around their self-published books. For example, most people who self-publish a cookbook are planting a tree in the middle of a very deep forest. Others, however, might tie their book in with live cooking demonstrations, relationships with food or grocery outlets, media appearances, and building an online community. Here as well, the point isn't just being an author - it is about building a brand and a business.

*If you are willing to learn the ropes and do the hard work of creating an information business around your writing, good luck and go for it! My focus in this chapter, however, is on your *writing* career. And in my opinion, whether you plan to self-publish or not, the best thing you can* *do for your writing career is learn your craft well enough to have the option of attracting a traditional publisher.*

When self-publishing makes sense

In fairness, self-publishing does have several advantages over traditional publishing. First, you generally keep a much higher percentage royalty from the sales of your books. Second, depending on who you work with, it is usually much easier to get or keep the rights to your work. And there is no question that you have much more control over bringing your product to market.

For many authors, these advantages are often dwarfed by the prospect of much smaller sales, or the need to depend on yourself to generate demand for your book. But there are some cases where it makes perfect sense to publish yourself. Here are some of the more important ones:

A well-established sales channel. If you write books that sell in large quantities to a particular market, self-publishing is often much more profitable, because you keep a much larger share of the royalties. For example, if you are a motivational speaker and sell hundreds of books each time you speak, or have a captive audience in your specialty, cutting out the middleman can make good economic sense.

A niche market. Major publishers are generally seeking books that will sell in quantities of at least several thousand copies. If your audience is small, self-publishing can be a legitimate and profitable way to reach that market. This does not necessarily preclude royalty publishing, however: even small markets often have specialty publishers or small presses with good sales channels into these markets.

You need a book for a book's sake. Here we are talking about meeting a specific business need, not simply the desire to be published. In general, self-publishing a book and then calling yourself a published author is still viewed a little like awarding yourself a trophy for a race you never won. But in many fields like public speaking or consulting, it can make sense to have a book that you sell at events or use to market your brand. In situations like these, self-publishing is often a legitimate and time-honored business practice.

You are simply that good. Some very successful authors, like Seth Godin in business or Hugh Howey in fiction, have built up very loyal "tribes" of followers. Godin was a bestselling royalty-published author for many years when he turned to self-publishing in 2012, funding his first project via Kickstarter and reaching his goal within three hours[4]. Howey went in the other direction, selling the paperback rights to his highly successful self-published fiction series (and keeping the e-book rights), eventually financing a lifestyle of writing as he sailed the world[5]. Once enough people like and follow your work, self-publishing can make a lucrative career even more lucrative.

Finally, let's look at what many people consider to be the principal argument for self-publishing: the idea that if your book is good enough, people will buy it no matter what.

I am just one small data point in the middle of nowhere, but in my case this hasn't been true at all. My nine nationally-published books have largely sold well, while sales of my two self-published books barely register. I was, in my humble opinion, a good writer for all of them. And the market even agreed: my first self-published book, a business fable adapted from a successful non-fiction title, was chosen as a book club selection by *Forbes*. But from a sales standpoint, it barely broke even. Same with my second self-publishing project, a collection of my communications skills blogs.

---

[4] Kleinman, Loren, "Why Seth Godin Self-Published," BookBaby Blog, May 19, 2015, http://blog.bookbaby.com/2015/05/why-seth-godin-self-published/

[5] Wikipedia contributors, "Hugh Howey," https://en.wikipedia.org/wiki/Hugh_Howey

Your mileage may vary. And at the end of the day, your own path to publication is a very personal decision. I respect whatever you choose to do with your own books. But if you want to sell books in large quantities, my advice will always involve being good enough to attract a major publisher.

"Fine," you are thinking to yourself. "Just go ahead and write a nationally-published book. Like telling a musician to go have a hit record. Easy for him to say." But bear with me nonetheless. In my view, if you write reasonably well – and more important, study the market – royalty publishing is well within reach of mere mortals like you and me. It is a choice you can make, and a goal you can work toward. Read on, and we will open my playbook on how to do this.

CHAPTER 7

How to Write Like a Published Author

Landing a book project with a publisher is a little like reaching the major leagues of a professional sport. The numbers are similar: several hundred people get to put on a major league baseball uniform every summer, while perhaps a few thousand new authors end up on the shelves of major bookstores each year. Sound disheartening? To the contrary. While you certainly need to have talent, the vast majority of newly-published authors are mere mortals like you and me, and your chances of success are surprisingly good - if you write well and take the time to learn how the business works.

So how do YOU get to the big leagues of publishing? Let's break it down. First, let's take three reasons some people incorrectly *think* lead to getting published:

You're famous. Nope. Not even close. I was a humble lay middle manager when I inked my first major book contract. A good platform helps, but many major CEOs can't get arrested in the publishing industry, while many of the hottest-selling nonfiction authors (like Harvey Mackay, who prints envelopes for a living) have day jobs no better than yours.

You've got connections. Interesting theory, but the facts don't bear it out. Most successful nonfiction authors are publishing industry outsiders, and I certainly am. For that matter, working with, hanging out with, or even being married to agents and editors doesn't carry much sway.

You've invested a lot of money. Many book-promotion gurus would have you think so. To be fair, marketing partners can make a difference, particularly when a book launches. But good books still find publishers, and crappy books with large promotional campaigns are still crappy books that don't sell.

Now, let's look at what I feel are the main reasons mere mortals (like you and me) do get published:

You have great content. Ultimately, people get published because *their books contain information people want to buy*. How to lead better. How to be happier. How to lose weight. How to win friends and influence people (sound familiar?). Good - and ultimately publishable - books always start by filling a need somewhere.

You write a *lot*. When I first started writing seriously back in the 1980s, you could have papered the walls of my room with rejection slips. Today, I rarely pitch a book proposal that doesn't eventually end up in a bookstore. What is the difference between then and now?

Simple: I stunk back then. I don't stink as much now. And the difference between point A and point B was paved with lots and lots of writing. The good news? Writing is fun. Or at least it should be, if you are going to do enough of it to become a publishable author. I had a lot of fun pitching innings in the minor leagues until I was good enough to be publishable, and all of it sharpened my axe as a book author.

You play the game by the rules. Here is where this chapter comes in. There are unspoken norms in this profession, and if you follow them, agents and publishers are much more likely to take you seriously. And if you don't follow them, you aren't in the running.

This latter point is perhaps the most important one of all: it forms the basis of smelling like a published author to people in the trade. Read on and you will see what I mean.

The five percent rule

Picture two musicians. One is a student of the music industry as well as a talented musician, and knows all about auditions, demo tracks, gigs, and how to relate to people in the business. The other stands, trumpet in hand, outside of Carnegie Hall, hoping someone will notice him and make him a star.

Which one do you think is more likely to succeed?

Book publishing works in much the same way. It is not a closed fraternity of insiders that doesn't welcome new writers – to the contrary, thousands of new books are published each year by royalty publishers. But there are norms you must follow to be welcomed into the club, and a surprising number of aspiring writers don't bother to learn and follow these norms. So our goal in this chapter is, truly, to help you smell like a published author and bring your goals of placing a book much closer to reality.

First, understand that book publishing falls under the larger category of what I call "the five percent rule." It applies to any desirable goal that many people are after, whether it is becoming a successful athlete, dating an attractive person or publishing a book. Here is how I would describe this rule:

Most people's chances of success are small – but most people who are serious, professional, and learn how the game is played eventually do succeed.

The five percent rule particularly applies to book publishing because the average book proposal does, in fact, have roughly a five percent chance of getting accepted by a publisher or agent, according to industry sources such as *Writers Market*.

But here is why that is the case: that vast majority of book proposals **stink**. More than half, according to my longtime literary agent. They are poorly written, have no discernable market, or don't fit the agent or publisher's list at all. Get rid of these smelly proposals – and multiply the good ones by the number of agents and publishers out there – and your chances rise to a more reasonable 50/50 in my view.

Now, let's get specific about how to be in the successful 50 percent. In my experience, your success pivots around three things:

- Writing a strong query
- Creating a book proposal that not only sells your book, but follows the norms of the profession
- Getting your query in front of the right people

Let's take a look at each of these in more detail.

Writing a strong query

The most important part of writing a book isn't writing a book. It's writing a one-page letter (or, more accurately, e-mail) known as a query. Write a great one, and your chances of getting to write the book go up substantially. Write a stale or trite one, and it doesn't matter if you're Kurt Vonnegut. If you can write strong queries, you can invariably count on book editors and agents asking to see your work – which, in turn, moves you much closer to landing a publishing deal.

I personally use a short, one-page query with three bullet-item paragraphs in the body of it:

- What the book is about: including its title and target market.

- Why this book is important: a quick, one-paragraph competitive and market analysis
- Why I'm the right person to write it: a summary of my writing and business credentials that are relevant to this book project.

That's it. No gimmicks, nothing cute, and no beating around the bush – just a short, readable summary of benefits that can be scanned in 30 seconds or less. Master this genre, and you will dramatically boost your success for writing in any other genre.

A sample query

Here is an example of a successful query that eventually landed me both a literary agent and a contract with a major New York publisher:

Dear ,

I am writing to seek representation for my sixth nationally published book project, entitled Beyond Attitude: The Psychology of Peak Customer Experiences.

ABOUT THE BOOK: Beyond Attitude is designed to do for customer transactions what the New York Times bestseller Crucial Conversations did for conflict management - present a literate, well researched look at the behavioral psychology that drives customer interactions, while giving readers specific communications tools that dramatically change the success of these interactions.

TARGET AUDIENCE: This book is targeted at the high end of front-line service professionals and the people who manage them. Its methodology has created dramatic real-life results including near perfect customer satisfaction levels, near zero turnover, and high sales growth. Its approach is now being incorporated as part of a campus-wide customer service initiative at Cornell University, and has been taught to thousands of people nationwide.

ABOUT THE AUTHOR: I am a full-time writer and corporate trainer with an award-winning 20+ year career in the software and call center industries. My five nationally published books include The Soul of an

Organization (Dearborn, 2002), which reached the Amazon.com top 2500 and was serialized by the Chapter-a-Day Business Book Club, and Smile Training Isn't Enough, an alternate selection of the Doubleday Executive Program Book Club. Perhaps most importantly, I am a consummate professional who cooperates with editors, promotes creatively and aggressively, and never, ever misses a deadline!

If you are interested in considering Beyond Attitude, I have a full proposal ready to send to you. Thank you very much!

Best regards, Rich Gallagher

This query was originally sent via e-mail to approximately 30 agents in early 2004. (I was "between agents" at the time, following the passing of my previous agent, and my placing my previous book directly with a publisher.) Of these 30 agents:

- *15 sent a rejection letter by e-mail, most within 48 hours.*
- *8 never responded.*
- *7 asked to see a copy of my proposal*
- *2 of these agents eventually offered to represent it.*

The agent I selected then sent my proposal to an initial group of 12 major business publishers, 10 of whom rejected it, and two of whom (Simon and Schuster and AMACOM) were interested in it. We chose AMACOM because of their track record with customer service books and their overseas distribution channels. I signed a contract in November 2004, and was given until mid-May 2005 to finish the book (which I did, at 5 AM, two days before the deadline :).

The book then went through a round of editing by AMACOM before being published in 2006 under the title Great Customer Connections. It reached a peak rank of approximately 8200 on Amazon.com, was reviewed in Business Week and much of the customer contact trade press, and was released in Europe and Asia by McGraw-Hill, where it was their 26th top selling trade book that summer.

Here is the single most important point about your query: the gut test. You must bring your "A" game here, and your idea and your title both need to ROCK. If your gut doesn't agree, or you know you are trying to stretch an idea into something publishable, you aren't ready to submit it yet. Your query needs to go POW — and if it doesn't, keep workshopping it until it does.

The principle behind a query is simple: does your idea excite someone about publishing your book? I can think of few other fields where just one page, properly written, can open the door to success. Which means that if you master the art of a good query, your odds of success go up dramatically.

Creating a winning book proposal

The *lingua franca* of nonfiction agents and publishers is a book proposal: a 30 to 50 page summary, market analysis and chapter sample of your book. Create a successful one, and you stand your very best chance of being offered a contract to write the book itself. And frankly it is a great system for you, the author, because you get to sell your book before actually writing it.

You don't normally send this proposal out cold to agents or publishers — that is the job of a good query. Queries respect people's time and get your ideas the up-or-down answer you want. But if people are interested, you must have a proposal locked and loaded to send them immediately. A proposal which, most importantly, will now be welcomed and read by the people you are pitching.

Remember the unspoken, dirty secret of nonfiction publishing we discussed earlier: the vast majority of book proposals are *terrible*. They pitch books that are poorly written, tone-deaf to the market, and will never sell. Which means that if you nail the art of the successful proposal, you - yes, you - stand a better than average chance of being on real bookshelves around the country.

A downloadable sample proposal from one of my own successful book projects is available online at the following link: http://bit.ly/2D5k8wo. Here are some of the key elements of a successful one:

1. Synopsis. This is the pitch for your book — one to two pages describing the core idea of your book, and its benefits to the reader. It needs to positively sing, particularly on the first page, because this is often scanned quickly to make an up-or-down decision. In particular, your title will do much of the heavy lifting for that all-important first impression.

2. Chapter summary. A quick list of the sections and chapters of the book, to give an idea of how the content will be laid out. (Note that you will be providing a detailed chapter outline later in the proposal.) As with the synopsis, the purpose of the chapter summary is to give an agent or publisher a quick overview of the book's content. Here, it is extremely important that your chapter titles "sell" the content and benefits of the book.

3. About the author. A one-page description of who you are, and why you are the right person to write this book. Be concise and punchy – this is not the place for a deathless laundry list of all your accomplishments since fourth grade, but rather a quick summary of your professional and publishing qualifications. This is no place to be shy and humble: toot your horn proudly and shamelessly here.

In this section, pay particular attention to your "platform" – your public presence in the media, the press, on social media, and as a public speaker. Platform has become an increasingly important criterion in recent years for placing a nonfiction book with a major publisher, because they want to know how large a "tribe" you can attract to purchase your book. All is not lost if you currently have a small platform: the strength of your experience and ideas may still carry the day. (And platforms are often built in the first place on the strength of a successful book.) But any track record of speaking, media exposure and/or business success can add a lot of value to your proposal.

4. Competitive analysis. Next to your synopsis, this is far and away the most important part of your proposal – so much so that agents and editors may check it first – because it is here that you will answer their single most burning question: "Will it sell?"

Here you will define the target audience for your book, and compare it to other existing books on the market. The gold standard for a good competitive analysis is that you have something new to offer *in a field of books that already sell successfully.*

The worst thing you can have in this section is a "unique" book with no competition – and the next worst thing you have is a book that is designed to be read by "everybody." These are both red flags for a poorly thought-out proposal. Make sure that you have a large but well-defined target market for your proposed book, compare it with at least 3-5 recent books that are still selling well, and have a clear and well-articulated benefit for your book versus the competition.

Pro tip: Don't bash competitive books in your proposal. First, it is considered to be in poor form. Second, and most importantly, proposals often end up in the hands of the publishers of these competitive books, particularly if you are submitting it through an agent. Your tone should focus on how your great book will improve on all of the other great books out there.

5. Project scope and marketing. Here you will discuss the specifics of your book – such as its length and wordcount – as well as what efforts you will add to market the book and help make it a success.

For the first part of this section, the most important thing is to be genre-specific and make sure your book fits the parameters of what is on the market. For example, the sample proposal linked above was developed at a time when popular business books tended to weigh in at the range of 200-250 pages or so, so I designed mine to fit the genre. (Nowadays, in an era of social media, blogs and information on demand, similar books tend to be shorter.)

For the second part, some of you may be scratching your heads and thinking "Doesn't the publisher promote the book?" The answer is yes, sort of. Understand that the goal of most publishers is to sell books, NOT to make you a star. This means that their efforts generally start – and end – with making your book available in normal bookselling channels, (briefly) building awareness, and then letting the market decide how successful you are. Some of the things a major publisher is likely to do include:

- Pitching your book to major bookstores (not every book from a major publisher ends up on the shelf)
- Promoting your books to sales channels such as libraries and book clubs
- Seeking media mentions through their contacts with magazines, newspapers, and (less commonly) television and radio
- Seeking subsidiary rights sales of your book, such as audio and foreign language editions

Now, here is where you come in. It is largely up to you to leverage this book for individual platform promotion – this includes things like speaking engagements, media appearances, guest blogs, social media, and book signings (which, incidentally, are generally poorly attended and horrible ways to market most books). Understand that things like book tours and media tours are reserved for a publisher's hottest new releases, which probably won't be you at first. So publishers expect you to put substantial skin in the game for book promotion, and this is the section where you sell what you will do.

The $298 book tour

When one of my first trade books was published – a text on managing software customer support operations in the 1990s – I had a pipe dream of having a West Coast book tour. And I actually made it happen.

The year it was released, the major software customer support industry conference was being held in San Francisco. I asked my publisher if they could help support a book selling and signing event there, and they offered to pitch in $250. I checked and found a discount $298 air fare from my home in upstate New York to San Francisco, somehow managed to convince the publisher that my book was worth an extra $48, and it was game on.

I truly made the most of that $298. I arranged a stopover with my parents in Arizona, stayed with them, and did some local publicity there – then I also stayed with friends in the Bay Area for the conference. We had a very successful signing event, selling out 100 books and getting some additional print publicity. But most importantly, I was able to tell people that my publisher flew me to a West Coast book signing!

6. Detailed outline. Here is where you start to get into the meat of the book's content. If an agent or publisher is still reading at this point, you have done very well, and the ball is on the goal line. But you still need to close the deal on the strength of your content.

I have always used a simple formula for my detailed outline: one page per chapter, with a couple of paragraphs describing the chapter content, followed by bullet items describing the "subheads" or specific points of the chapter. The end product should be a "mini-book" giving the reader a pretty good sense of your content and message.

7. Sample chapter(s). Next to the most important question ("Will it sell?"), the next two most important questions will be "Can you write like a published author?" and "Are you a sane, functioning member of society?" They usually will be able to tell both after reading a few pages of your stuff. Study other published authors, see how they structure their chapters and key points, and work hard to smell like one of them.

Normally one or two sample chapters will suffice here. (In my sample proposal, this was my third book for this publisher, so I simply provided one chapter.) Usually, your two chapters should be the introductory chapter (so they can see how the book will start) and a "meat" chapter from the body of the book (so they can tell if you are delivering what the book promises).

Finally, here are four "no-nos" that you should be careful to avoid as you prepare your book proposal:

Me, me, me: Your own story is really interesting – to your mother. The rest of us need actionable advice that applies to *us*. The sooner you talk about us readers, the better.

Misplacing the "Enter" key: People have really short attention spans. So please don't write sample chapters with paragraphs that run three or four hundred words a pop – this is the literary equivalent of making readers hold their breath underwater too long. Come up for air every 75-150 words or less.

Where's the beef: I have actually seen entire books – self-published, of course – wait until the very last chapter to divulge the "meat" of the subject. After pithering around for 200 pages or so describing the subject, explaining it, telling you why it is important, etcetera. Don't make the same mistake with your proposal. Both your pitch and your sample content should go "pow" and hit people right between the eyes, starting on page 1.

I don't need no stinkin' proposal: Far and away, the worst thing you can do to write a book is ... write the book. There is a reason that agents and publishers take on non-fiction books based on a proposal. You see, they want to know how likely your idea is to sell – and have a say in the content – before they even start worrying about your bon mots. So writing too much is actually just as a bad as writing too little, and will brand you as an amateur.

If you've been dreaming of becoming a published author, sweat the details in these specific content areas. And of course, before you get started, study the format of good proposals from reference books and even some publisher websites. Those who do usually get published eventually, and those who don't usually don't. It's as simple as that.

CHAPTER 8

Marketing Your Book Project

After all the hard work of developing a good, tight query and a strong book proposal, the actual marketing of your book project is usually much simpler than you think: you email your query to agents or publishers, and you wait. (And perhaps get moving on your next project.) Here are the key steps:

Step 1: Agent or publisher?

I've used the term "agents and publishers" frequently here, but not interchangeably. When should you contact agents and when should you contact publishers? This is a decision you need to make up front. And the answer depends on both your goals and the markets you are submitting to.

Not all royalty publishers are the same. There is a top tier of publishers – such as Harper Collins, Crown, St. Martins Press, and the like – who will not talk to mere mortals like you or me, and require submissions to come through an agent. You should only be playing in these waters if you have an extremely strong platform – for example, you are a celebrity, business leader, academic expert or popular public speaker – or have a stellar publishing track record. If this is you, your pitch will be to literary agents.

Then there is a wide range of publishing houses that welcome good book queries directly from talented authors. These include houses such as New

Harbinger Press (one of the largest psychology self-help publishers in the nation), O'Reilly (for technology-related books), and some mainstream larger publishers such as Wiley. In addition, depending on the nature of your book, there are specific markets such as specialty publishers, university presses, or small presses that may be appropriate for your proposal.

You may also be in the second category of author, but choose to seek an agent for the sake of using their services for rights, contract negotiations, and an ongoing relationship to place your current and future books. This is the category I personally fall in – I am not a celebrity, and my own books have all been with midlist and mid-major publishers, but I have worked with a top literary agent for much of the past 15 years. (As an aside, many of the books I ghostwrite have landed with top-tier publishers, because the credited author was a celebrity or had a strong platform.)

Timing is everything

Agents are somewhat harder to pitch than publishers – in part, because they are looking for good relationships with successful authors, not just good books. At the same time, their services can be invaluable in areas such as rights, contracts, and access to a wider range of publishers. In my view, a good agent is well worth the commission they charge for their services.

So even if your book is aimed at midlist publishers who welcome direct submissions, you may still choose to pitch it to appropriate agents – with one caveat: be sure to pitch your project to agents FIRST. If you submit to publishers first, and are not successful, you've poisoned the well for an agent – no one wants to take on a book and then discover that everyone has turned it down already. As the great comedian Milton Berle once said, "Timing is everything."

Step 2: Find your contacts

Now comes the fun part — coming up with a list of contacts to pitch your query to. This task is easier than you might think. First, subscribe to *Writers Market* (www.writersmarket.com), a continually updated online directory of publishing contacts and literary agents. It costs $5.99 per month or $39.99 per year as of this writing, and it will be the best few bucks per month that you will ever spend as a writer. Then search their listings to come up with potential agents and editors to submit to.

Keep a couple of very important things in mind as you prepare your list:

First, always get a name. Always! Even if a publisher's website tells you to submit to a department, such as "Editorial Department" — this is a one-way ticket to the slush pile. Writers Market or the publisher or agent's website often lists staff and their particular interests. If need be, you can even call the publisher and ask which editor handles your content area. (Once early in my career, when I called mid-major publisher AMACOM to get an editorial contact, their president Hank Kennedy answered the phone and actually spent a few minutes asking me about my book. Later I went on to publish four books with them.)

Second, do your research. Writers Market will provide a list of publishers or agents who claim to handle a specific area, such as business or psychology. Do not contact these people, however, until you do some online research using their websites, industry news, or personal directories such as LinkedIn.com. You may discover that your "psychology" publishing contact only handles books on specific topics, has moved out of the editorial side of the house, or is no longer with this publishing house. Or that they are not currently accepting new submissions. Or that another contact would be a better fit for your proposal. Nothing kills your proposal quicker than boneheaded submissions to the wrong people, so always look before you send.

Pro tip: Check sources such as the acknowledgements of competitive books, publishing industry trade articles or blog posts to find possible editorial contacts at your favorite publishers. Even if their email addresses are not listed, you can often use a publishing house's standard e-mail convention (john.smith@bigpublisher.com) to intuit it. And as mentioned above, there is usually no harm in calling and asking for contact information, particularly if you are polite and professional about it.

Step 3: Check for fit

Then there is the question of making sure that a book fits a publisher's list. Let's say that you write business books like me. Do you submit proposals to every business publisher? NO. Check out their other books first, particularly their recent releases. Some of them publish 150 page how-to books, and others publish 400 page academic tomes. Some are narrowly focused on, say, career skills and don't want to see your manuscript on strategic planning. Spend some quality time online (and, better yet, hanging out in bookstores) first and the rewards will come back to you many times over.

Step 4: Send it out

Once you have refined your list of potential contacts, your job is simple from here – email each of them your query. And then forget about it. Or better yet, get back to work. Some may respond, some may not (I personally wouldn't pester them again), and the market will ultimately have its say.

A proposal story

Back in late 2000 or so, I sent a pitch to several publishers for a book I was developing called The Soul of an Organization. It was about the core values that drive successful companies. And one of these publishers responded – their vice-president called me and mentioned that it sounded interesting, as long as it wasn't just another book discussing Fortune 500 companies.

*Oops. My proposal *did* mainly talk about Fortune 500 companies. So I went on the literary equivalent of a three-day bender, contacting every successful small business I knew and told them I need to talk to them NOW. And after a long weekend and lots of rewriting, I had a revised proposal ready to send them.*

*Unfortunately, they still decided to take a pass on my proposal. Then, another publisher came along and expressed interest in my query – and this time they *did* want examples from major companies as well as others. Another three-day bender ensued, and this time I was successful. The resulting book was published in 2002, reached the Amazon.com top 2500, and helped launch my consulting business.*

Pro tip: If you would like the opportunity to meet with agents or editors face-to-face, some writers' conferences offer paid opportunities to make your pitch in person – normally in a time slot of 3-5 minutes or so. Understand that these people will still accept or reject your pitch based on the strength of your idea – and that even if you are asked to send your materials, the answer may still be "no" back at headquarters. But if you feel making a personal connection might help your case, and you are comfortable making a presentation, this is another option to consider.

Some people also approach editors at events such as publishing conferences. The main industry conference, for example, is the Book Expo America (BEA) conference normally held each summer in New York. Admission to BEA requires industry credentials (although, with a little creativity, many people can get in through channels such as having a self-publishing imprint).

Should you approach people at shows such as BEA? It happens, and I have seen people make pitches there (in some cases, barging in during meetings between me and my editor). And I have seen one of these pitches get successfully placed, although most were not. BUT remember that editors are there to do *their* business – e.g. sell their current books – and you are interrupting their work. My advice? I feel that with a good query and proposal, your chances are just as good going through normal channels – so between that and the risk of making a bad impression by pestering working editors, I would normally take a pass.

Finally, some closing thoughts on the submission process:

Can you submit simultaneously? YES. Especially when a query is involved. It frankly isn't fair to your time, or theirs, to wait in sequence for one person after another to respond – especially given that some of them will never respond. Just be sure to be frank with everyone that this is a simultaneous submission.

Don't call us, we'll call you. Editors look at unsolicited phone calls from writers the way you look at telemarketers – only worse, because there are so many wannabe writers, so much work to do, and so few hours in a day. So while writing to an editor with a query is accepted (and, in fact, often encouraged), learn to see telephone queries for what they really are for most editors – an opportunity to guarantee that they will never, ever want to work with you.

Consider small markets. Legendary comedian Groucho Marx once said, "I don't care to belong to any club that will have me as a member." Professional writers think exactly the opposite way. You have a place on the publishing food chain – whether it is a small how-to book publisher or a major agent-only house – and you will have your best success pitching to publishers who already publish people with your kind of platform and experience. Aim for where you are welcome right now, and watch your credentials grow and your markets get bigger over time.

Buyer beware

In your search for a publisher, you are more than likely to run across royalty publishers who aren't quite royalty publishers. Once upon a time, they went by the name "vanity publishers" – you paid them a chunk of money, and they delivered you a garage full of copies of your book and wished you well. Today, you will hear terms like "cooperative publishing," "hybrid publishers," and the like.

These arrangements generally involve the author shouldering much or all of the financial risk of publishing a book in exchange for higher royalties. They may talk about having strict acceptance criteria, or substantial editorial or promotional involvement in your book. And many major publishing houses now have imprints where you pay to play.

I am not opposed to paying to publish your book. Some of these publishers provide a valuable service to writers who have the money and know what they are getting into. For example, I am aware of one pay-to-play publisher that has a strong word-of-mouth reputation among professional speakers, because they have a good track record of placing their books in places like airports and business bookstores.

That said, some other such publishers have a less stellar record. Some of the complaints about them include shoddy editing, poor communications, high fees, or lackluster marketing efforts. In some cases, getting the rights back to your book to publish elsewhere has been a tug-of-war. Overpromising and underdelivering is a fact of life for some of them. And in my humble opinion, getting published by most of them is not the same as landing a royalty book contract.

My advice? First, understand that with a traditional royalty-published book, they pay you. I believe that money should normally flow towards the writer, not away from him or her. And I still feel that most authors should aspire to write the kind of books that attract an advance and royalties. Second, if you decide to play in these waters, do your research. There are some very good firms and some truly bad actors out there, and opinions abound online about both. Good luck and caveat emptor.

CHAPTER 9

The Million Dollar Writing Life

n this closing chapter, we will take a look at some of the practicalities of freelance writing as a business, and a way of life. First, we will look at the economics of different kinds of writing. Then we will explore how you can leverage your writing career to bring in additional streams of income. Finally, we will close by discussing how writing is not just a way to make money, but a noble craft that continues to grow and evolve.

The economics of writing

How much money can you make as a writer? Sometimes, the answer seems like "how long is a piece of string?" But in reality, we can break down much of the economics of both freelance writing and book publishing, so that you can make an intelligent decision about where to invest your efforts.

First, let's take a look at freelance writing for others. I would describe the economics of this field in terms of a pyramid:

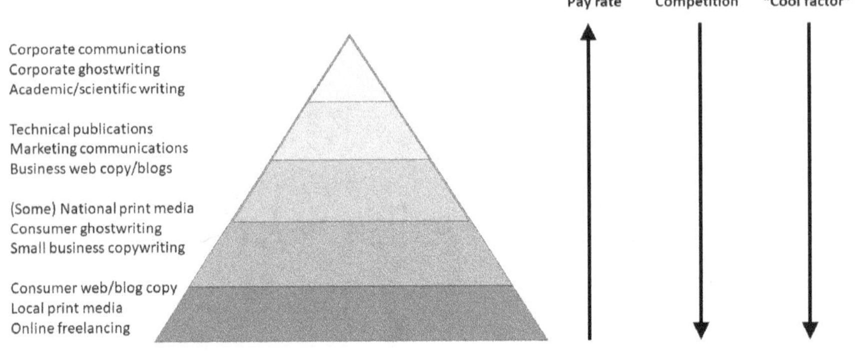

Notice something interesting about this pyramid? The higher the pay rate, the *less* competition you often have. Think about it: want to publish an opinion piece in your local newspaper, or a blog post in the *Huffington Post*? Both of these markets pay nothing at all, but competition is intense. How about a consumer magazine? Competition may be less intense, but when you factor in the time you spend querying, writing, and the relatively modest amount of pay involved, you are going to have to write a LOT of lifestyle pieces to purchase that new SUV, or pay your rent or mortgage.

This is why the popular conception of a writer is of someone bringing in a second income – and why I frequently get asked the extremely patronizing question, "What is your day job?" But keep climbing the pyramid, and things start to change. People who work in corporate communications or technical documentation often have legitimate, family-supporting jobs. Same with people who freelance in areas like these. And yet the door is wide open for people who want to do this work, because it lacks the "cool factor" of venting your political opinions, giving relationship advice, or interviewing a rock star.

So let's get specific here. How much can you make doing professional freelance writing? For one view of this, get on to Google and search "Writers Market" and "freelance rates". You should find a very specific, detailed article that breaks down current rates for various types of writing. Be aware that these figures tend to be on the high side, and may not be competitive in your market – God bless 'em, they are sticking up for fair compensation for our craft. But they will give you a good idea what to shoot for.

I'll be glad to give you a peek at my own pyramid. As of this writing in 2018, here are some of the rates I've been offered for various kinds of writing:

- Article in *Time Magazine*: nothing. (They approached me. I did it anyway, for my reputation.)
- Interview article in local newspaper, including photograph of subject: $50
- Spending two days editing a sample of a student's PhD thesis, and coaching them how to edit the rest: about $25 an hour, out of respect for the student's budget. (Students have no money.)
- Writing operators manuals for a local manufacturing firm: $50/hour
- Ghostwriting: $65/hour
- Corporate writing and blogging: $68/hour
- Academic writing and editing: $75/hour

So guess where I've spent most of my time? Yep. The last three have represented the vast majority of my income. And my clients have kept me very busy. Do the math, and I've made a very good income for someone living in a small town in upstate New York. So my advice for you? CLIMB THE PYRAMID.

Add in some of my other sidelights – being a public speaker and trainer about my own books, and later a part-time practicing psychotherapist (something that was always on my bucket list), and I did very well indeed. Most people here in my hometown have never heard of me, but I have always lived like a doctor or lawyer with a nice house, vacations, and new cars for my wife and me every three years or so. And more recently I retired early with no debt and no mortgage.

Disclaimer: The rates listed here are *my* actual rates. I can successfully charge these rates because I am experienced, I have a track record, my clients know me, and I am very good at this. (In particular, I write very fast and deliver a lot of content for a client's "hour.") And remember, these are "boring" specialty markets where I've developed expertise and a portfolio.

If you are just starting out and try to charge the same rates without the same credentials, you may not be competitive or successful at getting gigs. My advice? Find out what rates are in your market, and if possible, start *lower* than these rates so that you get gigs – and experience. Then raise your rates as your reputation grows. I pitched a lot of innings in the minors to get where I am, and you should too.

The only bad news here is that freelance writing income is *active* income: you earn money by the hour or by the project. You can't sit back and watch your freelancing income grow to a million dollars without doing a million dollars' worth of work. But with the right approach, it can become a stable, upper-middle-class income for good writers who pursue appropriate markets.

Now, let's turn our attention to book publishing. Most book publishing income is *passive* income: you write a book once, and then your income is proportional to how many copies it sells. This sounds great, in the sense that one book could technically sell a million copies and make you rich. But it probably won't.

To put this in perspective, one year I checked the sales figures for the year's top 10 selling business books (the genre I usually write in). The top book sold half a million copies or so – a nice payday indeed. The book in second place sold around a quarter of a million copies – or at typical royalty rates, about a $100K income for two co-authors. Then it declined rapidly from there. By the time we got to number 10 on the list, we were no longer talking about sales figures representing an upper-middle-class livelihood. And we are talking about the top 10 books of the year in a major nonfiction category!

Here are some other facts about published books:

- The average per-copy royalty for a published book is often less than a buck per copy. Typical royalty rates are less than 10% of the "net price," which is a steep wholesale discount from list price.
- Only a small fraction of published books ever sell more than 5000 copies.
- Sales of most books tend to drop off substantially after the first year.
- Relatively few books ever recoup the advances publishers pay for them. (Don't worry, you normally don't have to give it back.) For many if not most royalty publishers, a few very successful books make the profits that carry the rest of the books in their catalog.

So why bother writing books at all? For three important reasons:

First, a royalty published book from a major publisher is one of the very best credentials you could have as a freelance writer. It is like being in the major leagues of professional sports: it opens doors and opportunities for you, because you have proven you are one of the elite.

Second, it does pay. Given the economies of scale of a large publisher, five-figure advances and sales in the thousands are not uncommon. So your efforts in writing a successful book can still be cash-positive.

Third and finally is an issue we will discuss next: becoming a nationally published author opens the door to other related streams of income, which can be very lucrative unto themselves. Many people make much more money BECAUSE OF writing books than they will ever make FROM writing books – including myself.

Now, let's look at some of these potentially lucrative ways to make even more money as a writer.

Alternative streams of income

Earlier in this chapter, I mentioned that my top end as a freelance writer is roughly $75 per hour as of 2018. But how would you like to make $2500 an hour from your writing?

About 40 or 50 times per year, for close to a decade, I got up in front of audiences large and small to speak about the subjects of my books: how to handle your very worst customer and workplace situations. In some cases, I would be paid up to $2500 along with all-expense-paid travel to deliver a one-hour keynote speech to hundreds of people – sometimes being met at airports with limousines and put up in luxury hotel suites. And some speakers do much better than this.

This is just one example of how you can turn your writing into alternate streams of income. They don't involve writing directly but leverage your work as a writer to open doors that otherwise might not have been open to you. Let's look at just a few of these avenues:

Public speaking. People will always want to learn new things and be entertained. If you have knowledge to share, you can make people laugh, or you can motivate them, the stage may be the place for you.

You do not need to be a royalty published author to start building a platform as a speaker, but depending upon your topic, it can give you a substantial leg up. For example, when my book *What to Say to a Porcupine* became a national #1 bestseller in customer service, offers to speak around the United States came pouring in – it was like winning a game show. And many speakers go in the opposite direction – they build their reputation and platform skills first, and then as their popularity grows, they create traditionally published or self-published books to further build their brand and audience.

If you are interested in following this path, start developing your topics and platform skills locally and then build from there. Organizations like Toastmasters International – often referred to as "the off-Broadway of speaking" – often have friendly local meetings that help people learn to speak, along with regional meetings and competitions. Speak often – and in many cases, for free or small honoraria at first – and build your skills and word-of-mouth reputation. While developing a full-fledged speaking career is beyond the scope of this book, a great place to start is Lois Creamer's 2017 book *Book More Business: Make Money Speaking*, as well as the National Speakers Association's flagship book *Paid to Speak* (featuring a chapter from yours truly on book publishing).

Organizational training. When you are a professional writer, you often have expertise that helps people work better – including how to write better! The training market in North America alone is currently more than US $150 billion per year and continues to grow. And unlike professional speaking, you don't need a big platform or an audience of hundreds to have lucrative gigs.

I personally have done a great deal of organizational training in areas ranging from customer service skills to stress management, all leveraging books or other publications I have written. These gigs have ranged from small workplace training sessions to leadership retreats for senior executives. To get started, speak with the human resources or training departments of area companies, or the business extension of your local university or community college.

Writing workshops and retreats. If you write professionally – and particularly if you are a published author – your expertise is often valuable to people who want to build their own writing skills and careers.

I first got my start as a writer at one such workshop. I was a software engineer in the 1980s, had recently taken over as the editor of our small company's newsletter, and wanted to learn how to write better. I attended a weekend workshop taught by an award-winning children's book author, where we learned the basics of writing for publication and got feedback on our own work. Her advice truly helped launch my interest in writing professionally, along with a community college writing professor who encouraged me to pursue it further. Whether you organize these workshops yourself or find a sponsoring organization, sharing your own skills can be a win-win for both yourself and the people you teach.

Individual coaching. As a professional writer, you can often play a valuable role in helping other people one-on-one to learn to write better, or sharpen their work to make it ready for publication.

Google "writing coach" to see examples of other people, locally and nationally, who serve the public. Increasingly coaches serve a broad audience online using email and videoconferencing, and one source lists rates ranging from $30-300 per hour.

One caution from my own personal experience coaching writers, however, is to be selective about clients and projects. While most clients are great, I have occasionally been approached by people with pretty crazy ideas and crazy personalities, because writing attracts people from all walks of life who feel it may bring them fame and fortune. Screen carefully, and caveat emptor.

Information products. As a writer, you also have the opportunity to take your expertise and turn it into products that can help other people, such as workbooks, audio courses, videos, online self-help programs, and others. You are benefiting from one such product right now!

This is just a sample of some of the possible ways you can turn your writing skills into additional sources of income. Just like with your writing, follow the lead of the marketplace and look for specific needs you can fill. Writing is a profession the revolves around communication, and you can often leverage these communications skills to help others as part of a successful consulting practice.

In closing: Never stop learning

In the Middle Ages, monks and scribes labored for months to create books written painstakingly on parchment made from animal pelts, using quill pens and scraping knives for corrections. Today, writers create large amounts of content on demand using their word processors and desktop publishers. The common denominator between both of these groups? A noble craft that has helped enlighten the knowledge of the world.

If there is any closing advice I can give you in your path as a professional writer, it is to never stop learning. This is a field that is always growing and evolving. As someone in my 60s as of the late 2010s, I did my first writing on a manual typewriter, and today I do most of my work electronically. And I have watched the tastes, preferences and markets that drive the writing profession continue to change every year.

So as you hopefully grow and succeed in your own writing career, never stand still. Keep up with the field through publications, blogs and social media. Network with other writers. Attend conferences. Treat your work like the profession it is, and be an active part of it, like I still do.

As we reach the end of our journey together, I hope you have learned some real, practical tips and techniques that will help you join me in what I feel is one of the best ways to make a living – being a professional writer. Best of success!

Bonus #1: 25 Hot Freelance Writing Markets

Here is a list of 25 potential places to find your next writing gig. It is designed to help you get a *fast* start on your freelancing career, by helping you focus your portfolio development and prospecting efforts.

There are three important things to know about this list:

- *First, it is organized by the job functions of people to approach, not by the type of writing.* This is because I want you to focus on potential markets to contact. This means that this list will overlap in the types of writing involved: for example, you may develop blogs for marketing agencies, corporate marketing, non-profit organizations, professional practices, and many others.

- *Second, this list is designed to help you target your market.* There is often safety in numbers: the bigger a market is in your area, the better your chances are of getting your foot in the door to land freelance assignments. This, in turn, can inform your prospecting efforts. For example, if you live in a place like Silicon Valley that a crawling with technology firms, it may make sense to focus your portfolio and prospecting efforts on areas like technical documentation or courseware. Conversely, if there are only a few such firms in your area, you may find they all have staff or dedicated freelancers already – and you might focus on a market that is broader where you are.

- *Third, it focuses on aiming high in your contact strategy, such as the head of a department or function.* In general, it is usually better to aim too high versus too low, because a more senior person is likely to direct you to the right place – perhaps with a personal recommendation. But use your judgment: for example, if you are trying to write for a huge organization like Ford Motor Company, you may not be able to get past the gatekeepers for that entire company's director of marketing, and will probably want to research and cultivate contacts in specific project areas.

Pro tip: What about marketing online?
You will find that the focus of this guide is on local people you can approach in person. Why? Because your very best success in prospecting for freelance work generally lies in arranging to meet with people face-to-face. Relatively few people land high-paying freelance writing work using purely online marketing.

Ironically, once you land freelance writing relationships you can often work electronically for them from a remote location. Moreover, your current clients often can make warm introductions between you and clients in other places – many of my current clients are in fact remote, and some have never met me. But I believe that at the high end of the market, initial client relationships are largely built in person.

Now, here's the list. Good luck!

1. Temporary help agencies. I am mentioning this first, because it is often one of the best places to start when you are first launching a freelancing career. First, the barriers to entry are frankly often lower for new writers – agencies are often under pressure to deliver manpower quickly, on demand, when a client project crops up. Second, the kind of gigs that would go through an agency often last weeks or more. Third, you have the opportunity to build relationships with both agencies and their clients (as long as you respect the agency's rules for working directly with clients – often a buyout or non-compete period is involved.)

How to approach: Find agencies that place technical or business writers, create a good portfolio to show clients, and get on the agency's roster.

2. Product manufacturers. What does nearly every manufacturing facility in your town have in common? The need for written information about their products, ranging from manuals on how to use or service them to sales and marketing materials. Better yet, small-to-medium sized firms often can't afford to hire a writer, because they do not have enough volume to justify hiring even a part-time one. (Which makes you the perfect candidate.)

How to approach: Create a portfolio of your best work, contact the marketing and engineering groups of these firms, and start knocking on doors.

3. Software documentation. Technical writing in general is a rich motherlode of freelancing in areas that have a sufficient number of firms, with the software industry taking a lead role. This is because nearly all kinds of applications software need documentation to support how to use it – and these needs often come in waves, making it very appropriate for freelancing. To succeed in this area, you do not have to be a software expert yourself, however you must be able to make its usage clear for potential customers who will be using it.

How to approach: it will be important to develop a portfolio of similar documentation first, particularly since you will be approaching many prospects about being available for a future need. For smaller software firms, approach product development management or company management directly, while larger firms often have a technical documentation department that can use freelancers for peak periods.

4. Hardware documentation. Everything that we just said about software documentation above also applies for technical and instructional materials for hardware products, ranging from circuit boards to mechanical devices.

How to approach: Use a similar contact strategy as for software documentation, including having a targeted portfolio and approaching product development or documentation management.

5. PhD students. What stands between students at the highest level of academic achievement and their degrees? A thesis that often runs hundreds of pages. Which may be the first major thing they have written in their lives. A good editor can help focus their content, and turn their research and deathless prose into a real publication with a beginning, a summary, and actionable conclusions. Be sure you understand academic thesis requirements such as APA or Chicago style manuals and citation formats before you play in this market.

How to approach: Contact faculty who work with graduate students – most thesis editors are recommended to students by faculty. You can also advertise in places graduate students read, such as online newsgroups and student publications.

Pro tip: When doctoral students have no money, offer to edit one chapter of their thesis, and then show them what you did and how you did it. Everyone wins and you build a good reputation.

6. University faculty. Professors must publish or perish. Unfortunately for them, and fortunately for you, not every talented faculty member is a good writer. Be prepared to keep your relationships confidential and ethically appropriate. (You can edit their content, but you can't do their work for them.) The need to publish over a lifetime career often makes these good long-term relationships.

How to approach: If you knock on the doors of professors and offer to write for them, it might be awkward and embarrassing on both sides – because the public perception is that they should already be accomplished writers.

But they always want and need writers who can help their students edit their doctoral theses, so these faculty can get them off their back and graduate. So approach faculty about editing PhD theses – or perhaps other funded consulting projects they are working on – and subtly mention that you do other academic writing as well. They'll get the hint.

7. Government contractors. The Federal government produces massive amounts of written content every year – everything from research publications to web sites to consumer advice, and everything in between. To a lesser extent, the same is true for state and local governments as well. Some of this content is produced in-house by government employees, but a great deal of it is created on a project basis by freelancers. And because government agencies often have ongoing projects, they can be a great source of recurring work. I personally have made a great deal of my freelance income from writing and editing government publications.

How to approach: The GSA has a search tool that you can use to determine what firms have currently been awarded GSA contracts, the GSA E-library (https://www.gsaelibrary.gsa.gov/). This will provide names of firms you can research and approach for potential freelancing opportunities.

Pro tip: Cracking the government market
Note carefully that we are talking here about approaching "government contractors," not the government itself. Why? Because dealing directly with the Federal government as an independent freelancer is not for the faint of heart, and beyond the scope of this book. It involves everything from bidding on contracts to becoming registered as a GSA (Government Services Administration) contractor, often with stiff barriers to entry such as a minimum volume of business. So always remember that *you are generally marketing your services to contractors who bid on government contracts, not to the government itself.*

Numerous firms exist for the sole purpose of landing and servicing government contracts. In the Federal government arena, many of these firms are based in the Washington DC metropolitan area and are known informally as "Beltway bandits," named after the interstate surrounding the DC area. And at a broader level, many large firms – particularly in the defense and "Big 4" consulting space – serve as government contractors.

8. Advertising agencies. These firms help organizations sell their products and services, by telling a good story about them to potential customers. Their efforts can include areas such as advertising copy, media spots, blogs, social media, and other areas. Some of these are boutique agencies serving small business, all the way to larger firms targeting corporate clients, and they are often clustered in major cities.

How to approach: For smaller agencies, contact the head of the agency directly with samples of your work. For larger ones, research contacts who manage the development of creative content (often known in the trade as "creatives").

9. Marketing agencies. To the untrained ear, advertising and marketing agencies may sound similar, but they have very different functions. Advertising involves copy designed to sell products to consumers or businesses, while marketing agencies support corporate visibility and branding efforts – often involving channels such as blogs, websites, and videos. These firms often serve organizations who outsource some or all of their marketing content to a third party.

How to approach: These agencies tend to be small – for firms under 200 employees, approach the president or CEO directly.

10. Web designers. Firms that are hired specifically to develop websites for clients often need the services of a talented writer to create copy or content for these websites. You will often need to be comfortable using common web design tools such as WordPress.

How to approach: Develop sample content using a web design platform, and approach these (generally small) firms directly.

11. Medical and pharmaceutical writing. According to one published paper, medical writing has become the fourth most outsourced form of writing, and has more than doubled between 2005 and 2010 to over a half-billion US dollars in annual revenue[6]. Projects range from regulatory documents for pharmaceutical manufacturers to clinical research papers for health care professionals. The bad news? This isn't a field for amateurs, with specialized knowledge of both the field and its publications needed — many practitioners have graduate science degrees or industry expertise.

How to approach: Developing a portfolio of experience is essential for this field. Marketing contacts include the documentation departments of larger firms, consulting firms specializing in this area, and larger research institutions.

12. Financial writing. The finance and banking industry is a large consumer-facing business, ranging from boutique investment firms to large multinational corporations. Their needs range from marketing materials and blogs to assistance with research reports on specific companies or markets.

How to approach: Contact the management of smaller firms directly, or the marketing or publications departments of larger firms.

13. Corporate finance. The central corporate functions of an organization are responsible for publications such as annual reports, which are periodic and demand-driven needs that are often required by law.

How to approach: Consider building a portfolio through projects with small or non-profit organizations. To market yourself, contact the corporate finance or controller's office of target organizations.

14. Corporate communications. This function revolves around creating written content, often on short notice. Their deliverables include press releases, news stories, and official company statements. The bad news? This function is often staffed in all but the smallest organizations. The good news? Many firms supplement their staffs with talented freelancers, and

---

[6] Sharma, Dr. Suhasini, "How to Become a Competent Medical Writer?", Perspect Clin Resv.1(1); Jan-Mar 2010.

some small organizations may be open to outsourcing this function to a freelancer.

How to approach: Start building a portfolio by preparing sample press releases for yourself or small organizations, and publish them using free or inexpensive channels such as *PR Newswire*. Then approach managers of corporate communications.

15. Corporate marketing. Mainline corporate marketing departments are one of the primary sources of writing work within an organization, developing materials such as blogs, white papers, solution sheets, and web copy.

How to approach: Make sure your portfolio includes good examples of marketing collateral, and sell your ability to turn products and services into a good story. Contact the director of marketing in most organizations.

16. Corporate editing. This is primarily the domain of small organizations – particularly technical ones that do not employ full-time writers, and would benefit from turning what their engineers and technical experts write into publishable content.

How to approach: Your target market consists of people who produce written material for non-expert customers, written by expert staff. Generally this falls under the wing of a firm's marketing department. Here, your portfolio should focus on before-and-after examples of good rewrites, as well as the speed of your work.

17. Professionals who speak. Speechwriting is a very specific, targeted market. It generally doesn't include full-time public speakers: while some may quietly employ a ghostwriter, the vast majority develop their own content and platforms. (And often, give the same performance over and over for different audiences.) However, many professionals find themselves having to speak as part of their jobs or platforms – and having a niche for creating these speeches quickly and professionally can fill a real need. Your key skills here is to get into someone's head and work quickly, using a minimum of their time – and being able to tell a good story matching the timing and pacing of the spoken word.

How to approach: Your audience here includes mid-to-upper level management, C-level executives, and academics with a public or national platform. Start with small gigs and develop a portfolio around this specialty first. In particular, videos of successful client speeches will be an important marketing tool.

18. Video production firms. Some firms specialize in producing corporate or organizational video material, for promotional or instructional purposes. These projects often involve video scripts that are read by teleprompter, versus just turning on the camera and "winging it."

How to approach: Contact these firms directly with samples of your work.

19. Book publishers (freelance editing). Two people approach a major book publisher. One of them pitches a book project. The other offers to provide freelance content editing and copyediting for their book projects. Guess which person is much more likely to get the gig, and which one usually makes more money per year? Yep, the latter. Any organization that produces large written projects – like books, reports, monographs, and the like – needs editors.

How to approach: If you are a stickler for detail, and the kind of person who is always silently correcting everyone else's grammar, this is your gig. Build a portfolio of before-and-after projects, get the names of editors or editorial staff, and ask to be part of their freelancer list.

20. Non-profit organizations. "But non-profit organizations don't have any money!" Yes – that is exactly the point. More than most markets, the non-profit sector needs writers who can help organizations *raise* money – such as writing grant proposals, copy for fundraising letters, and political advocacy.

How to approach: Build a portfolio through low-cost or donated work, gain testimonials that focus on what kinds of financial results you've produced, and target organizations you can help to grow. Go directly to the CEO of smaller organizations, or the marketing department of larger ones.

21. Courseware developers. Many products cannot be sold without training courses on how to use them. These include software programs, complex machinery, or specialized equipment. Courseware is often a good niche, particularly with multiple clients, because needs are episodic and timed with product releases. To develop effective courseware, you will need to be comfortable developing presentation materials (using software such as PowerPoint or Keynote), student workbooks, and exercise materials – which means learning how to use these products yourself.

How to approach: Depends on the size of the organization. For smaller firms (under 200 employees), courseware development often falls under the wing of product development teams, so you will approach people such as directors of software development or manufacturing. Larger organizations tend to have a formal technical documentation or training development function handling this (*not* the same as corporate training, which coordinates internal training for a company's employees).

22. Ghostwriting. We devote a whole chapter to this in the main book. For now, understand a few facts of life. First, most aspiring ghostwriters need to have some book projects under their belt – for example, by publishing under your own byline, or helping to develop a book as part of your job. Second, you need to understand the publishing market well enough to deliver market-appropriate, publishable projects to your clients.

Finally, realize that only bigger fish can afford you: senior executives, successful speakers, top academics, and the like. Think of how much it would cost to hire a plumber or even a lawn mower for as many hours as it takes to write a book, and you get the idea. (Ironically, a good ghost often pays for him or herself when a successful book sells well or is placed with a publisher. But only at the top end of the market, not with your next-door neighbor's novel.)

How to approach: Ghostwriters do not knock on doors. The likelihood of contacting someone at the exact moment they want to publish a book is close to zero. You will generally market yourself via your website, articles, contacts within the communities you might write for, and word-of-mouth from satisfied clients.

23. Professional practices. Customer-facing professional practices such as law firms, larger medical practices and others often need marketing collateral, blogs or other promotional material to build their reputation or explain their services. Size is important here: a three-person doctor's office is less likely to have regular needs for content, versus a large multispecialty practice (although not impossible, if for example they blog regularly or have a strong marketing presence).

How to approach: Focus your portfolio on appropriate promotional material such as brochures, blogs, or client/patient information material, and approach the heads of these practices directly.

24. Service businesses. This is a niche market for the right kind of freelancer. Service businesses ranging from plumbing firms to insurance agencies have needs that include advertising copy, blogs, web site copy, and a social media presence. They tend to have sporadic needs for content owing to their size, so your marketing efforts here will involve casting a wide net for a large number of clients. However, this can be an effective market in areas where these service businesses are a big part of the local area, particularly for larger ones.

How to approach: Approach these businesses directly, and focus on how you can make them look good and increase their sales.

25. Extension services. Agricultural or cooperative extension programs exist to provide information to the public, on subjects ranging from farming to health, homemaking and leadership. Much of this information is created in the form of documents, web pages or other forms of written communication.

How to approach: In the United States, cooperative extensions generally exist at the county level. The National Pesticide Information Center (NPIC) maintains an online directory of these offices at the following link: http://npic.orst.edu/pest/countyext.htm

Pro tip: What about freelance job sites and consumer publications?
You may have noticed the conspicuous absence on this list of online sites seeking talent for freelance writing gigs, such as eLance, Fiverr and others – or consumer publications. Why is that?

In my case, personal experience. I have never really had much success getting freelance writing gigs from online sites, and more important, they seem to focus on low-paid gigs with a great deal of global competition. Likewise, articles for consumer publications may look good on your resume, but competition is fierce and pay rates are often very low. If you want to become a million dollar writer, my sense is that these channels are not the way to get there.

(Ironically, I have written articles for major consumer publications such as *Time Magazine* and others, but usually for free – and because they approached me as a book author. In these cases, I have written such articles for the sake of my platform, not my income.)

I have no doubt that some freelancers get gigs, or even perhaps carve out a living, using the online marketplace or by writing for the consumer press. Succeeding in this environment undoubtedly requires working quickly and aggressively, building a platform and getting good client ratings, among other skills. But my focus is on helping you get highly-paid, regular writing work you can build a lucrative career around, and my personal belief is that there are better places to look.

Bonus #2: 60-Day Freelance Writing Action Plan

One of the biggest problems with getting started in the business of freelance writing is … getting started. It is often a major career decision, with many details involved. So it is very easy to get paralyzed wondering what to do next, and never quite get off the ground.

The purpose of this document is to help you break down the startup of a real freelance writing business into actionable steps that you can take over the next 60 days – eight weeks in total. It will help clarify your most important steps and serve as a guide to developing your personal business plan. You should refer to this document often as you get started, to make sure you are on track.

First, there are three important caveats for using a tool like this one:

- *Your timeframe may vary*. In this case, the term "60 days" is a metaphor, not a rigid guideline. You may choose to spend more or less time on the individual components of this plan, change their order, or skip steps entirely. Moreover, your time horizon for starting a business may vary – you may want to ramp up cautiously over a long period of time, while others may choose to take a flying leap into their first major paid gig. It is OK to choose whatever timeframe and pace that makes sense for you.

- *Know your level of risk tolerance.* Some people may feel very good about making an immediate transition to freelancing – for example, they are already in a secure retirement, have a substantial cash cushion, or have a good fallback position if they fail. Others may not be in a position emotionally or financially to risk the loss of even a single paycheck. Just because you *can* start a business or *plan* to start a business does not mean you necessarily *should* do so, because success is not guaranteed. I personally am very risk-averse, and started my freelancing business as a rational alternative to unemployment after a restructuring at my previous employer. For others, moonlighting or starting gradually may make more sense, particularly if you have secure employment. Know who you are first, and think through what level of risk makes sense for you.

- *Success depends largely on you.* Have you ever met one person who works hard and succeeds at their goals, while another complains bitterly that they have "tried everything" and can't succeed? There is a large matrix of factors in the success of any individual: their attitude, their social skills, their competence, and the amount of time and effort they invest in their craft. Here is a reality check for anyone who wants to make a living as a writer: you have to be able to write extremely well, adapt your style to a client's needs, have very good people skills, be comfortable with technology and the online world, and be creative and flexible in finding clients. And frankly, have the ability to look in the mirror first when something needs to improve. There must also be a large enough market in your area for what you are offering. Finally, there is no substitute for lots of hard work.

The good news? If you love to write, know you are good, and keep learning and growing, much of the hard work you will need to do to succeed won't *seem* like work. I personally pitched lots of innings in the minors on the way to building a successful consulting practice, but truth be known I enjoyed every minute of it. And with a good plan under your feet, you can often succeed that much faster.

My hope is that this planner will become part of the game plan for your success. Good luck!

Day 1: Creating a vision

Many people wake up in the morning dreaming of making a living as a writer. Today, you are going to take an important step beyond those dreams – you are going to capture in writing what specific goals you are going to go after, and how you plan to get there.

Take out a sheet of paper, and ask yourself the following questions:

- What will my successful life as a writer look like?
- What will I be doing two years – or five years – from now?
- What kind of writing do I want to specialize in?
- What kinds of clients will I approach?
- Will I be doing this part-time or full-time?
- Will I start this business while moonlighting at something else, or devote my full attention to it?
- Do I have support of my family, friends, and partner?
- How much income do I plan to make?
- How did I arrive at this income figure? Have I checked market rates for what I want to do?
- Are there alternative streams of income I want to pursue from writing, like speaking or training?
- How will I be financially secure while I build this business?
- Can anyone serve as a mentor to me as I get started?
- What will I do if this doesn't succeed? Broaden my scope of practice? Try something else? How long can I invest in trying to make this work?
- What is my one-sentence summary of who I am and what I do?

Dreams are important. But when you start getting the specifics of these dreams written down *on paper*, you start the important process of turning these dreams into a game plan.

Pro tip: If possible, get feedback on your vision for this business from the people who know you best, such as your friends, your co-workers, or your partner. You may find that everyone is in agreement about your plans. OR you may find that people who know you well can see possible roadblocks or issues for you to consider. (Bonus points if these people understand the practicalities of the writing business.) Either way, feedback can be extremely useful to you at this stage.

Understand that at the end of the day, you are still the person making the decisions. Don't let people be dream killers if you know and trust yourself better. (You should have been a fly on the wall when I told my family – all of whom have engineering degrees like me – that I was going to give up a perfectly good technical career to become a writer.) But listen with an open mind, and see how much the input of other people resonates with you.

Week 1: Develop a plan

Next, we are going to take the results of the good brainstorming session that you had on Day 1, and start turning it into a plan for action. There are two important reasons for this step:

- First, this plan will start guiding your efforts in the days and weeks to come.

- Second, creating this plan in the first place will serve as a reality check on your ideas. (One of many reality checks to come, by the way.)

For example, let's say that you are a former marketing professional, and you want to focus on writing for corporate marketing departments. If you discover that there are only two small potential clients in your area, something needs to change – either your scope of practice, the geographic area you serve, or perhaps something else. This week we are going to "road test" your ideas from within the comfort of your home.

For the rest of this week, your mission will be to take the ideas you wrote down about your business and flesh them out into detail. Here are some of the tasks you will do:

- Research actual potential clients in your chosen market(s).
- Create a list of potential prospects, including job titles and names if possible.
- Identify possible mentors or colleagues who already do this for a living (and if possible, arrange to speak with them as soon as possible).
- Do a detailed financial analysis of your cash flow during your startup period.
- Examine potential alternate sources of income as you ramp up.

At the end of this period, review your findings, and see how it informs your original plan.

Week 2: Sweat the practicalities

When you are starting a business, you are not only the CEO: you are the finance, HR, marketing and custodial department as well. If your analysis from the first week tells you that it is time to move forward with a professional writing business, now is the time to take care of some of the more important practicalities of this business – because your business and its structure must be in place before you start prospecting, signing contracts, or invoicing clients.

Here are some of the things to focus on as you set up your business:

Business name: What would you like to call yourself? Many freelance writers simply go by their name, or use the form "My Name and Associates" – even if the associate is your spouse or is furry and has four legs. Alternatively, you can choose a business name that either creates an emotional image for your customers, sells the benefits of what you do, or emphasizes your niche – or whatever else you wish. (Note: I personally have always practiced as "R.S. Gallagher and Associates.")

Pro tip: Most freelance writers keep their business name simple – and usually go by their own name, because if you remain a solopreneur, eventually *you* will be your own brand. Trying to appear bigger than you are can actually work against you (many if not most potential clients hire individual freelance writers), and getting too cute with your name could confuse people about what you do. But follow your gut and choose a name that best fits how you see your business.

Business form: Your choices here include a sole proprietorship (where you are the sole owner, and your business income is reported as personal income), a partnership (where one or more partners are involved), a limited liability corporation (LLC) or S-corporate that combines corporate liability protections with pass-through income, or a regular corporation. In any of these cases, you will generally need to register your business with state or local authorities to be able to open a business checking account and accept payments under your business name.

Which form is appropriate for you will depend on your personal financial situation and potential liabilities, and is beyond the scope of this book – consult your lawyer or financial advisor to discuss your specific situation. Personally, I use an LLC to shield my personal assets from possible business liabilities, while keeping my financial accounting as simple as possible.

Web domain: Whatever you call yourself, people will need to find you on the Internet, particularly once they start doing business with you. Claiming your "real estate" on the internet in the form of a web domain name is fairly straightforward – go to a domain registrar such as GoDaddy or Network Solutions, search for the name you wish, and if it is available, sign up to claim this name for what is normally a modest annual fee.

Pro tip: If your favorite domain name isn't available – such as your name or business identity – consider using a different top level domain (such as .net or .me instead of .com), using your middle initial, or appending something like "writer" or "writes" to your name. (In my own case, Rich Gallagher is a very common name – there are nearly 300 of us on Facebook alone – and RichGallagher.com was long taken by the time I started consulting. So I use my first and middle initials, to have the top level domain "RSGallagher.com")

Email address: Once you line up a domain name, you have a lot of flexibility in creating email addresses using that domain name (for example, "george@georgewriter.com"). Alternatively, you can create a business email identity using public email services such as Google's Gmail or Yahoo (like "georgewriter@gmail.com").

Phone number: It is generally a good idea to have a separate business phone with its own voice mail or answering machine – nothing spoils that professional business image quicker than having your 12-year-old pick up the phone! There is generally no need to get fancy with things like custom or toll-free numbers, as long as customers can reach you. Some writers use a dedicated cell phone as their business phone, others use a "distinctive ring" to bundle a separate number on their home phone, while others use newer voice-over-IP (VoIP) services that allow access to calls and voice mails online.

Banking: Once you have set up a business identity, including your contact address and phone number, be sure to set up a business checking account allowing you to invoice and receive payments from customers. For many writers, it will be important to accept direct deposit payments from clients and wire transfers (for international clients). In the latter case, being paid by wire transfer can help avoid onerous exchange fees for checks issued in foreign or Canadian funds.

Pro tip: Online credit card processing services such as Square or PayPal Here have revolutionized your ability to accept credit card payments, and are usually very easy to set up. Most business clients still prefer to pay via check or direct deposit, to avoid paying credit card processing fees, however credit card capabilities can make it easier to work with small clients and/or public events such as selling books.

Weeks 3-4: Develop your portfolio and your business presence

For the next two weeks, your primary mission will be to develop the materials you will need to call on prospective clients, as well as respond to potential business inquiries. These include:

Your portfolio: Your ability to land clients will depend in large part on the impression your writing samples leave. The most important factors here will be (a) the quality of your writing, (b) the look and presentation of your samples, and perhaps most importantly, (c) how well your portfolio targets the niche(s) you are prospecting in.

The importance of credentialing yourself in a niche cannot be overemphasized – it is truly the secret to success at the high end of the freelancing market. Suppose you live in Silicon Valley, and decide to specialize in creating software documentation. If you call on software firms with a portfolio of general business writing, the odds are that you will never be called back. However, if you have a sharp-looking portfolio of attractive software documentation samples, and let numerous companies know that this is your specialty, it would be hard to imagine NOT landing gigs over time – and the same is true for most niches with sufficient prospects and writing needs.

Pro tip: Is your past experience a little thin in the niches you want to move into? Consider creating hypothetical examples from scratch. There is nothing disingenuous about creating generic samples of your writing, as long as you are honest with potential clients that these are not real projects.

Your business card: You need cards to leave behind with potential clients and business contacts – and these are often easy to produce on your own computer and printer via template software if needed. There is no need to get too fancy here, but having a card that is clean, professional and attractive will make a difference in attracting clients.

Pro tip: Leave your picture off your business card – you aren't a real estate agent.

Business collateral: As with your business card, your other business materials – such as your letterhead, your marketing materials, and the folders or CD labels containing your portfolio materials – should reflect a common, professional business image. Many of these materials can be produced at home using your own computer and printer, and in many cases a small investment in professional printing can pay large dividends.

Week 5: Start prospecting

Now comes the fun part – contacting potential customers in your target market(s).

The basics of this are normally pretty simple: you contact potential clients by email and/or phone and request to meet with them, or ask your personal connections to make warm introductions to decision-makers for you. And then you wait, keeping in touch periodically with those who are potentially interested in your services.

Pro tip: Start with the low-hanging fruit
Many freelance writers begin their careers with gigs that are close to home – literally. They do projects for former (or even current) employers, relatives in a family business, or close friends or colleagues in the business or organizational world.

There is no shame in leveraging your personal connections to get started as a writer, and no loss of face in starting with projects from friendly sources. Each of these projects give you a chance to show off your talents, take their written materials to the next level, and build your portfolio.

Here are some guidelines for prospecting, particularly in the early stages:

-Get names. You are always selling to people, not job titles. A mass mailing to "Manager of Technical Documentation" at 100 companies is likely to produce zero results (yes, I've tried it), while a targeted personal contact to someone who needs what you offer is much more likely to be successful (and yes, I've tried that too – it works much better).

-Don't "sell." As of this writing in 2018, society is increasingly moving away from interruptive selling. And at a personal level, nothing will kill your business faster than appearing desperate or becoming a pest to potential contacts. You have just two jobs when you meet with a prospect: delight in their company and build a human connection, and show them what you can offer them. Then let nature take care of the rest.

It is OK to check in periodically with people, but not too often (and preferably through "soft" contacts – for example, an email sharing interesting news or data with a prospect is much more effective than a phone call wondering when you will get hired.) You generally cannot talk yourself into a future project, but it is far too easy nowadays to talk yourself out of one. And personally, some of my most lucrative long-term consulting projects have come from people who initially didn't respond to me for months.

-Give the process time. What are your chances of meeting with a prospect, and discovering that they need your help tomorrow and hire you? It almost never happens. (And when it has for me personally over the last 20+ years – very rarely – it has always involved warm introductions, not cold calls.) Play the long game – you are making contacts now that are designed to pay off weeks or months in the future, when a need arises that you can fill. Remember that gaining customers in the first place is much harder than keeping them, so set a goal of gradually building a pipeline that, in time, will hopefully keep you very busy.

Pro tip: You can't start a freelance writing business on Monday and expect to be busy by Tuesday – or worse, *need* to be busy by Tuesday. Always have a backup plan, savings cushion or other sources of income to give yourself the time and space to build a pipeline of clients.

Week 6: Refine your message and portfolio

As you start prospecting, you are gaining something that may even be more valuable than a future pipeline of clients – you are gaining valuable information about what people need, and don't need.

For example, you may be a financial professional who has decided to specialize in creating annual reports. But now that you are actually prospecting, you are discovering that no one needs annual reports, but lots of people need corporate newsletters. As you listen to projects, and hopefully learn from them, be open to making course corrections in your business materials and your portfolio.

Even more important is what I call the "gut test." How are prospects reacting to you? Are they receiving you and your materials with great joy, or tepid enthusiasm? Listen to them and read their body language. Even if they don't need you right now – which is more than likely – you should be getting feedback at this stage about how needed your services are. If you aren't passing the "gut test," you need to reexamine your niche – or step up the game with your writing – or both.

Week 7: First gig!

Congratulations! You have landed your first paid project, and you are off and running.

Your goal at this point is extremely simple and to the point: completely blow your new clients away. Beat their deadlines, preferably with gusto. Make their written materials look and sound spectacular. Be an absolute pleasure to work with. Welcome their feedback and criticism. When they ask you to jump, ask "how high?" And when things go wrong, remember that nothing is ever a problem, even if it is.

I can't overemphasize this point enough: your business will live or die on what kind of an experience you give your clients. I call it the Krispy Kreme principle: by making the perfect glazed donut and serving them hot to people, suddenly everyone realized that they needed more glazed donuts in their life. You want exactly the same thing to happen with your business. And frankly, people loving my work and finding more things to have me write for them was a huge part of my own transformation from a good consultant to a Million Dollar Writer.

Week 8: Renew, refresh, review

As you enter your eighth week of starting a freelance writing business, don't be surprised if you are starting to feel like you've been on spin cycle for a while. Between starting up your business, doing your initial prospecting, and actually doing the work with your initial clients, this is a very emotional and exhausting time.

Be sure to take time to take care of yourself, and be close to your family, friends, and the other people in your life. And take time to take stock of these first few weeks of this new business, and see how you feel – I call it having "a meeting with myself." Don't be afraid to be honest with yourself about what is or isn't working for you, and don't be afraid to change course if needed.

Day 60: Go for it!

For these last eight weeks, you have been on an incredible journey. You have set out to launch a business around your passion as a writer, and have gone through the steps of making it really happen. Congratulations!

So why did we choose 60 days, instead of 30 days, or 120 days, or two years? Because two months is a good time frame for learning if you are going in the right direction. You have hopefully learned what your niche(s) are, whether clients need what you are selling, and above all whether *you* enjoy doing this for a living. And however long or short it takes to fill your pipeline of clients from here, you should have a better sense by now of whether you will eventually get there.

(And on a personal note: when I ran screaming from corporate life for the last time many years ago, leaving my job without a net, it took roughly 60 days for me personally to line up my first gigs and know that my consulting practice was a going concern. Your own mileage may vary.)

If you truly love to write for people – like I do – my hope is that you are now seeing your way clear to a life that merges your passions and talents with your livelihood. Best of success!

Bonus #3: Guide to the Perfect Query Letter

They say that a journey of a thousand miles starts with a single step. And in much the same way, your journey to a nationally-published book project starts with a single page – your query letter. And this single page is perhaps the most important element of all in your project.

When agents and editors review your project, they don't need 100 pages of material to evaluate it. More than anything, it has to pass their "gut test," which usually has three parts: (a) do they like your idea, (b) does it fit their client list or catalog, and (c) will it sell?

Of course, only the market can answer the third question – however, publishing professionals can answer the first two immediately, and have a sense about the third as well. As soon as they see your idea, of course. This is where your query letter comes in.

A good query puts your idea out there for a quick up-or-down answer. And that is a very good thing. I know of no other profession where a single page can take you as far towards a substantial, paid project. But this means that every word of a query has to work hard for you, and you have to bring you "A" game to have a chance of getting a positive response.

This short document highlights the mechanics of writing a strong query letter. Do this well, and your success will lie exactly where it should – on the strength of your idea. Let's look at how to make your query letter a great one. Good luck!

Good query letters are hard to write, but easy to start: you present your idea, normally in the form of a book title, subtitle, and brief description. For example:

I am writing to query you on my latest book, *The Lettuce Diet: How to Lose 50 Pounds in the Next Week*. Studies have shown that eating nothing but lettuce causes people to lose weight faster than any other approach, and this will be the first major book to turn lettuce into a diet plan for rapid weight loss[7].

This opening can take other forms as well – for example, one popular one is the rhetorical question ("Did you know that 90% of children with head lice never finish college?") But either way, the first short paragraph or two gets the idea, the title and subtitle, and the benefits out there quickly.

In all likelihood, the decision to accept or reject your query will rest with how agents or publishers react to this opening. So let's break down its components in detail:

The title

I sometimes joke that you should spend at least twice as long on the title as you do on the book itself. But I am only partly kidding. The right title will literally make or break your book. For example, let's compare two books on the same subject: one is titled *Outsourcing Common Business Tasks*, while the other is titled *The Four-Hour Work Week*. Which one would you pull off the shelf?

This is a near-perfect example, because Tim Ferriss's choice of title had a great deal to do with *The Four-Hour Workweek* becoming a major international bestseller, which in turn helped launch his platform as an

---

[7] Note: This is, of course, not a real diet. It is a humorous and hypothetical example of a book proposal. Please do not try to lose weight by eating just lettuce.

author and expert. So let's look at some of the components of a successful title:

It leads with a benefit. In nonfiction, nearly every bestselling book has a title that puts a reader benefit front and center. Look at *Think and Grow Rich* or *How to Win Friends and Influence People.* – both of these titles date back to the 20th century but are still bestsellers today. Among more recent titles, you will find books like *The Ten-Day MBA* or *The Life-Changing Magic of Tidying Up*. In most cases the title tells you exactly why you should purchase the book, and how it will improve your life.

It is short and punchy. Very few titles are more than five to seven words long. A good title's job is to get in there, create a strong mental or emotional image, and then get out of the way.

Pro tip: In recent years, it has become fashionable to use a single word or punchy short phrase that captures the essence of the book, and then leave the details to the subtitle. For example, Gary Vaynerchuk's *Crushing It! How Great Entrepreneurs Build Their Business and Influence – and How You Can, Too*, or Tony Robbins' *Unshakeable: Your Financial Freedom Playbook*.

It sounds like a book title. This should be obvious, but for many rookie query letters, it sadly isn't. Popular nonfiction book titles have a sound, a rhythm and a cadence all of their own. When you read them out loud, they sound unmistakably like a book title. Get on to Amazon or go to a bookstore and silently mouth book titles to yourself – and then see if your title would join the club.

The subtitle

In a good query, you could view the subtitle as the brains of the operation: it provides the detailed pitch that will make your book idea seem attractive and reasonable. It represents your opportunity to sell and credential the book's idea. In a very real sense, it validates the promises made by its louder and more insistent cousin, the title.

Here are some of the key features of a subtitle:

-*Many start with action words*. The classic opening word of a subtitle is "How" – how to lose weight, how to be successful, how this amazing new principle will change your life. Other common action-oriented openings include words such as "Why," "Overcoming," "Healing" or "Solving."

-*Others describe the subject matter as data*. Another classic subtitle technique is to pair an active or provocative title with a description of the subject matter. Here are some hypothetical examples: *"Outrage! Leaving the Toilet Seat Up in Post-Gender America."* or *"The Lost Ones: When Teenagers Can't Find Their Phones."* Or perhaps a list of examples of the title's topic: *"Burp! Coke, Pepsi, and the Rise of Fizzy Soft Drinks"*

-*It sounds like a book subtitle*. Once again, subtitles have a length, rhythm and cadence that fit the genre. Study other nonfiction subtitles to inform your own choice of style and wording.

The description

Next, you should describe the benefits of the book within the opening paragraph or two. Here are some guidelines for making this sing:

-*Keep it short*. This should be no more than a short, punchy, benefit-laden sentence or two. Why? Because if you can't sell the benefit of a book quickly, no one will pick your book off the shelf. Editors not only want to hear about your book's benefit, they want to know that its pitch is a short burst of instant gratification.

-*Don't repeat the title*. Every word is precious in a query, particularly given that your first paragraph or two will make or break your chances. Provide more details to credential the premise of the book, describe its potential market, or (if you must) paraphrase the core premise of the book again. But let your title and subtitle do the heavy lifting of selling the idea.

-Sell the benefits. There is no need to be shy here. If this book will fill a critical market need, teach a needed skill, or change people's lives, this is the place to say so. The higher purpose of a book description is to sell how people will benefit from reading it.

Target audience

The worst possible audience for a book is "everyone" – niches matter. So use your next paragraph to describe, in as much detail as possible, who the book is intended for.

The best audience, of course, is a potentially large one that already purchases competitive books that sell. Whatever your target demographic group – new mothers, midlife career-changers, anxiety sufferers, music lovers, sexual abuse survivors, etc. – be sure to describe it in detail, including numbers if possible. ("This book is aimed at the 43 million people who prefer vanilla ice cream to chocolate.")

This section is also a good place to share any past experience you have had serving this target market, as part of your credentials for writing the book – including courses you have taught, successful projects you have done, audiences you have spoken to, and the like. Keep it short and focused on the demographic, but don't be afraid to toot your own horn here.

About you

The next paragraph has one purpose and one alone: to describe why you are the best person to write this book. It is a *short* summary of your qualifications, in a single paragraph (preferably) or very brief bullet list. Here you should mention things such as:

- Past experience
- Previous publications
- Media credits
- Speaking platform
- Social media presence
- Awards that serve as credentials (for example, a Book of the Year award is very relevant – a performance award at your workplace is not)

This section needs to strike a delicate balance. On one hand, you can't be at all shy here: you want to sell the idea that you are the ideal author for this book, and that a publisher would be lucky to have you write this book for them. And yet at the same time, you can't be boastful, vain, or drone on and on about your qualifications. Practice the subtle art of summary here, and let your real credentials shine through.

Pro tip: The About the Author section of the back cover of a book is a good example of the length, style and tone you are shooting for here. Study other book covers to get a sense for how you're the author description of your query letter should read.

The closing

Now it's time to wrap it up. Keep it short and simple here: if they are interested, you have a complete book proposal ready to send them.

One other important point about your closing is to include complete contact information in the signature block at the end of your email – including address, phone number (landline and cell if appropriate), email address, and website if applicable. This signature block gives agents and editors several ways to contact you, as they are most comfortable, and serves as one final selling point to your query package.

Pro tip: Five no-nos for book queries
Aside from what you should include in a query, there are a few things you shouldn't include as well. Here are some of the key ones:

Sales estimates: No one can predict how many copies a book will sell. Even publishers. Saying "this book will be a bestseller" brands you as an amateur and makes you look stupid.

Attachments: Tempting though it may be, don't attach your proposal to your query. Editors like to be *asked* to see your work first, and the convention is to send the proposal once they ask. Attaching it first comes across a little like showing up for a first date with a ring. Moreover, some email addresses reject emails with attachments, raising the risk that your query isn't seen at all.

Unsubstantiated claims: The key here is to let your title, subtitle, description and credentials do the talking. Evidence-based statements are fine, and perhaps important ("Studies show that 90% of students would like more information on dating"). And it is fine to make it clear that your book fills a need. But idle boasts ("This book will be the next *One-Minute Manager*") usually backfire.

Laundry lists: A query is not a resume. This is not the place to list all 45 articles you have published, a bullet-item list of your career accomplishments, or anything else that is long-form. Save it for the About the Author section of your book proposal.

A seventh or eighth paragraph: Queries are designed to be short and read very quickly – you will be fortunate if an agent or editor spends more than 30 seconds on yours before coming to a conclusion. Droning on and on will not leave a good impression, and will signal that you don't understand the genre.

Ready to go

And now, you are hopefully ready to send your query letter out! Queries are generally sent to agents and editors by email nowadays. Always send a query to an individual by name, not by job function (like editorial@bigpublisher.com) – even if publishers ask you to do this, be aware that this is often a one-way ticket to the dreaded slush pile.

Pro tip: if an agent or publisher responds positively to your query, send them your proposal *immediately*. **Never send a query letter unless your**

proposal is ready to go. Querying someone and then making them wait for you to finish brands you as being deadline-challenged in general, which is *not* a good impression to make when you are trying to land a book contract.

In general, some agents or editors respond quickly (often just to say "no" – it is a numbers game), others over the next 2-4 weeks, and some will never respond – my advice is to let them go and not pester them further. And if you are fortunate, one or more will respond by wanting to see a copy of your proposal. (In some cases, you may even get a phone call, so be sure to include your full contact information in your signature line.) By the time a month has passed from your initial query, you should know whether your efforts have been successful or not.

Good luck and best of success!

Bonus #4: Worksheets

This section provides supplemental worksheets designed to help you get the most out of the content you learn from this book. It covers areas including:

- Freelance writing market analysis
- Freelance writing marketing worksheet
- Freelance writing business analysis
- Book proposal competitive analysis
- Book style worksheet
- Book query template
- Book proposal template
- Book marketing worksheet

Each of these worksheets will help draw out the most important ingredient in planning your writing career – YOU. By putting pencil to paper, or finger to keyboard, you will make an important commitment to bringing these lessons to life, by going through these worksheets yourself with your own data. The results will then help form your personal plan for developing a business as a writer.

Putting these worksheets into action

Each of these worksheets has an instruction page describing the contents of the worksheet, followed by the worksheet itself. You can use these worksheets in one of three ways, depending upon your preferences:

- Make a copy of each worksheet – or the entire workbook – and fill the sheets out manually. This gives you the advantage of taking these tools with you wherever you wish, without the need for a computer.

Pro tip: Note that you can print as many copies of each worksheet as you wish, for multiple prospects, book proposals, etc.

- Copy the text from each worksheet into a document or spreadsheet of your own, so you can fill them out electronically on your own computer or tablet.

Pro tip: Copy the worksheet contents into a simple text file or word processing document first, then format them as desired in a reproducible document or spreadsheet.

- Customize the contents of these worksheets to suit your own particular writing markets and business needs – for example, describing subspecialties of a particular target market, or specific competitive points for a book project.

Pro tip: Consider using bold versus non-bold formatting, or different levels of indentation, to add subcategories to an existing worksheet.

Success in both freelance writing and book publishing are, more often than not, the result of a dedicated process. These worksheets will help you break this process down into small, achievable steps, and help give you a framework to take action.

Freelance Writing Market Analysis

They say that if you don't know where you are going, any road will get you there. This worksheet will help you avoid this in your freelance writing business, by planning where you intend to target your marketing efforts.

The purpose of this worksheet is twofold:

- First, it will help you analyze the market potential of areas that you might want to serve as a freelance writer. For example, you may discover that there is a wide range of potential prospect organizations in the area you want to write in – or that prospects are slim, and you need to broaden or change your proposed market, geographic area, or scope of practice.
- Second, it helps you create a list of target organizations to contact as you seek freelancing opportunities. In the next worksheet, we will drill this list down further into specific names and contact strategies.

Space is provided to list both local prospects you might approach and meet with in person, as well as remote clients you might approach electronically. Be aware that the latter represents a much more difficult sales cycle for high-value work, because high-value freelance writing tends to revolve around individual client relationships. However, if you have contacts or specialized expertise that might be attractive to specific remote clients, you are not limited to your local geographic area.

This worksheet also explores other potential sources of writing income, including temporary help agencies and other channels, as well as your perception of the market potential of your listed prospects. This market analysis will then inform all the other efforts that follow in building your freelance writing business, including developing a portfolio, branding yourself, and reaching out to potential clients.

Freelance Writing Market Analysis

I. About you

a. What market segments do *you* want to write for?

b. What experience or expertise do you already possess in these areas?

c. What geographic radius will you serve? Will you serve local clients, online clients, or both?

II. Potential prospects

a. List your prospecting criteria here. (Include factors such as organizational type, current headcount or annual revenue, market specialties, known writing needs, or other factors.)

b. List names of organizations in your *local* area that fit these criteria.

c. List names of *regional, remote* or *online organizations* that fit these criteria.

d. List the names of regional ***temporary help agencies*** or other channels that have recruited technical, business, marketing or other freelance writers within the last three months.

III. Market potential

a. Rate how you see the market potential of each of these organizations listed in section II, based on criteria such as the following:

(1) competitive barriers (e.g. how many people try to write for them)
(2) volume of writing you estimate they need
(3) perceived openness to freelancers
(4) ability to contact and meet with hiring authorities

Freelance Writing Marketing Worksheet

Once you have narrowed down the potential markets for your freelance writing services, and established potential client organizations, you can move forward with contacting potential clients.

This worksheet helps you log and track your contact plan, based on the target markets you have identified. It covers areas including what job titles or functions to target, approaches you will use for finding contact information, and your contact strategy.

Pro tip: Many small businesses use contact management software to keep track of their marketing activities, and many of these tools are either free or available at a modest cost. Consider integrating your results from this worksheet with a basic contact management system that fits your business and workstyle.

Freelance Writing Marketing Worksheet

I. Prospect targeting

a. For each organization you listed in your market analysis, list which *job functions* you will target in your prospecting search. (Example: manager of technical documentation, director of marketing communications, product development manager, etc.)

b. For each of these job functions, write down how you will try to obtain specific *names* to contact regarding your services. (Example: online search, professional directories, business-related social media sites such as LinkedIn, contacting client organization directly, etc.)

c. Are there any professional *activities*, such as conferences or networking events, that you can attend to discover and/or meet potential contacts?

II. Contact strategy

a. For each **name** you have identified, list how you intend to contact them. (Email, telephone, personal introduction from mutual contact, etc.)

b. Log the status of your contact activities.

III. Sample contact email

a. Create a draft of a sample contact email, introducing yourself and your work, and offering to set up an initial meeting with the potential client.

Freelance Writing Business Analysis

Setting clear financial goals is an important part of building a stable, successful freelance writing business. By knowing how much you need to make in what period of time, you can avoid falling into the trap of simply taking "the next gig" and losing track of your goals.

This worksheet will help you work backwards from the amount of time you have to work with, the amount of money you need to make, and what markets will best get you there. This doesn't imply that you must restrict your attention to the highest-paying markets – if you really want to make a living working with small non-profit organizations, for example, you don't have to write rocket manuals instead. But it is important to know how much income and how many productive hours will help you reach your goals, and this worksheet will help.

Freelance Writing Business Analysis

I. Financial goals

a. How much *income* do you want to make from freelance writing over the next year, and long-term?

b. How many *billable hours* do you plan to spend writing over the next year? (A full-time job normally encompasses 2088 hours. Also, remember that few if any freelancers are able to fully bill all of their time.)

c. What is the *average hourly rate* you will need to earn to meet your financial goals for the next year? Start by dividing answer (a) by answer (b), and then add a "margin of safety" to this estimate.

II. Market assessment

For each *organization* you identified in the previous Freelance Writing Market Analysis Worksheet, list what kinds of rates you can charge for freelance writing services. (Consult resources such as *Writers' Market*, temporary help listings and established local freelances for possible rates.)

III. Business plan

a. Discuss how your financial goals and market prospects will inform your business plan, and describe what prospecting and networking priorities you plan to follow as you build your freelance writing business.

b. Discuss how you plan to "ramp up" your business, and how you will sustain your livelihood as you build your freelance writing practice.

Book Proposal Competitive Analysis

When you are planning to write a book, one of the worst things you can do first is … write the book. Or even the book proposal. Why? Because your best chance of success in placing this book with a royalty publisher lies in first doing a good competitive analysis of other books that currently sell in your niche.

This worksheet will help you create a market-informed book proposal, by exploring the current competition for your book, and finding a niche that is appropriate to both your message and your current platform. Plan to explore currently selling books on Amazon.com or other sales channels, and/or what competitive books are currently on the shelf at major bookstores. (Preferably both!) Then look critically at how your book idea fits within the current competitive landscape.

Finally, understand the mindset that you should be bringing to this competitive analysis. Having competitive books in your niche is a *good* thing. No one will ever write the last diet book or self-help title – and conversely, being the very first book in your category is usually a much tougher sell. Also, see what books are appropriate to your platform. For example, if all of your competitors have national reputations and you don't, a simple tweak to your idea – such as adapting it to a niche market, or making it more of a trade or how-to book – may make your proposal that much more competitive. Good luck!

Book Proposal Competitive Analysis

I. Current market

a. Describe what kind of non-fiction book you plan to write.

b. List up to ***five current books in print*** that compete most directly with your proposed book.

c. What are the current ***sales ranks*** of these competitive books on Amazon.com? Do any of these books have sales ranks in the top 150,000 for all books?

c. Describe the ***platforms*** of the authors of these books (e.g. their positions, media profile if any, number of followers on social media).

II. Evaluating the competition

a. Are any of these competitive books successful (e.g. sales ranks in the top 150,000 on Amazon.com, or on the shelf at major bookstores)?

b. How does your platform (e.g. your media, speaking and social media presence) compare with competitive authors? Do any successful authors in this genre have platforms comparable to yours?

III. Impact on your proposal

a. What will be your book's unique contribution to this market niche?

b. If your book lacks successful competitors *OR* your platform is much smaller than these competitors, what changes might you make to your proposed idea to make it more competitive?

Book Style Worksheet

Once you have done a good competitive analysis, your next major decision before writing a book proposal is to decide on its style and format.

This is your opportunity to position your book against those that are currently selling, and thoughtfully choose a style that helps it fit better in its category. Planning your style ahead of time has some important advantages:

- Publishers instinctively tend to slot books into specific categories, and even have their own shorthand for these categories – for example, they will talk about something being a "seven steps book" (even if it actually has more or less than seven actual steps), or a thought leadership book. If your book fits one of their "slots," it is much more likely to get their attention.

- Having a chosen style can then serve as a personal plan for the development of your proposal and eventually your book, in terms of areas such as word count, chapter structure and story arc.

- The right style can help your book quickly gain mindshare within the reading public. For example, have you noticed that many science fiction authors tend to write trilogies, while very few ever write a "quad"? In much the same way, your book's style can serve as a sign that you belong in the "club" with other competitive titles.

This worksheet will help you break down your proposed book idea into reproducible elements of style, which in turn can then help guide your book proposal.

Book Style Worksheet

I. Overall style

a. What kinds of book style categories do you see among competitive books in the same niche as your book proposal?

b. Is there a specific style category you plan to choose for your book proposal?

II. Specific elements of style

a. Describe the style of your proposed book at a general level.

b. What is its planned word count?

c. How many chapters will it have?

d. What will its chapter structure look like?

e. What will the opening "hook" of the book look like?

f. How do you plan to open – and close – specific chapters?

g. Will this book be primarily written in first person (e.g. your opinions), second person ("you need to do this"), or third person ("here is how people do this")?

h. How would you describe the story arc of the book? (For example: premise first, followed by examples? A solution to a problem presented in multiple steps? Individual narratives? Etc.)

i. Do you plan to have a contributed preface or foreword? Whom do you have in mind as a contributor?

j. How will you end the book? With a summary of the content, a last "step," an epilog, etc.?

Book Query Template

Book queries are simple in form, but powerful in impact. They are a straightforward one-page summary of your book title, description, benefits, and your qualifications to write it. Normally sent by email to agents or editors, these queries represent the traditional way to gain an audience for your book proposal.

This worksheet lays out the elements of a typical book proposal, and will help you structure this important document around your book idea.

Book Query Template

I. Title and concept

a. What is the proposed title and subtitle of your book?

b. Provide a *one-sentence* description of what your book is about.

II. Reader benefits

a. Describe the benefits – and in particular, what *unique* benefits – that your book will offer readers.

b. Can you describe briefly – ideally in a sentence or two – what differentiates your book from its competition?

III. About the author

a. Using no more than one short paragraph, describe who you are and why you are the ideal person to write this book.

Book Proposal Template

A book proposal is the key document that will get accepted or rejected by an agent or publisher, and is your key to landing a book contract.

If you have been invited to submit a book proposal on the strength of your query, your idea has already passed the first and most important test. Now, this proposal will show stakeholders in the publishing industry how well you can carry through this idea at book length, and how well you write. Be sure to have a complete, edited proposal ready to go at a moment's notice before you start querying people.

This worksheet is designed to clarify your thinking about how you organize the key parts of your proposal, and should be followed in order. It is, of course, a summary for what will often become a 30-40 page document by the time it is completed. Use this template to identify your main points, and to refine the story you will tell to sell this project to others.

Book Proposal Template

I. The basics

a. What is the title and subtitle of your proposed book?

b. **Synopsis:** What are the key points you will make about your book here? (Pro tip: refer to the book summary you wrote in your query, and ideally open your synopsis with this.)

c. **About the Author section**: How will you describe yourself and your platform here?

II. Positioning your book

a. **Competitive analysis**: What books will you compare your book with, and what key points differentiate your book from them?

b. **Project scope and marketing**: What will be the size and chapter length of your book, and what activities (speaking, articles, local media, social media, etc.) are you planning to promote it?

III. Outline and sample chapter(s)

a. **Outline**: What are the sections and chapters you will list in your outline, and what key points will you make about them?

b. **Sample chapter(s)**: Which chapter(s) will you include as your sample chapter(s)?

Book Marketing Worksheet

After all the hard work of developing a good, tight query and a strong book proposal, the actual marketing of your book project is usually much simpler than you think: you email your query to agents or publishers, and you wait. (And perhaps get moving on your next project.) In addition to this, in some cases there may be other channels such as pitch events at writers' conferences.

This worksheet will help you detail your contact strategy, specific names to contact, and the results of your marketing activities. Use it to clarify the marketing plan for your book contract, and keep track of your progress.

Book Marketing Worksheet

I. Prospect targeting

a. Are you planning to approach agents or publishers with this project? (NOT both.)

b. Given your platform and competition, which publishers are your target publishers? (List these even if your goal is to place your book with a literary agent.) Will your target publishers require the services of an agent?

c. What types of books would your key editorial contacts normally represent?

d. Do you have possible contact referrals from friends or colleagues who publish successfully?

II. Contact strategy

a. List each *name* you have identified and plan to contact.

b. Log the status of your contact activities.

c. Are there alternate submission channels you plan to pursue, such as agent or editor pitch events at writer's conferences?

ABOUT THE AUTHOR

Rich Gallagher is a successful non-fiction author, freelance writer and ghostwriter. He has written nine royalty-published books under his own name, including two national bestsellers, one of which was a finalist for 1-800-CEO-READ's Business Book of the Year. He has also ghostwritten numerous books for major CEOs and academic figures, published articles for *Time Magazine*, CNN and other major media outlets, and built a successful business producing business and technical writing for clients worldwide. In addition to writing, Rich is also a successful public speaker and a practicing psychotherapist.